"*Mobilizing Men for One-on-One Ministry* is a huge win for the men of the church today! With the pressures we all face, we need other men to help us stay committed to finish strong for the Lord. This book will inspire us to take our growth to the next level together."

—**Dr. Tom Mullins**
Co-Pastor, Christ Fellowship
Church

"Having worked with men for over forty years, I believe Steve Sonderman's new book is a must read for every church, whether they have a men's ministry or desire to start one. Practical, biblical, and based on real life experience at Elmbrook Church over many years, his mix of principles and actually doing it move it from fiction to fact. This work is a true gift for the church."

—**Robert McCook**
Founder and Executive Director,
Priority One Foundation

"Men get lost without a map! Steve Sonderman has given us the map to know how to reach men for Jesus Christ! He knows the way! Now, we can have a tool to help us impact the lives of men with a transforming friendship and discipleship."

—**Stephen W. Smith**
Author of *The Transformation of
a Man's Heart, The Lazarus Life,*
and *Soul Custody*

"Steve Sonderman is a no-nonsense, hands-on, down-to-earth man's man. Just the kind of guy that men listen to. He writes the way he is—so men read what he writes too. Wise guys!"

—**Stuart Briscoe**
Minister-at-Large, Elmbrook
Church; Telling the Truth
Ministries

Books by Steve Sonderman

FROM BETHANY HOUSE PUBLISHERS

How to Build a Life-Changing Men's Ministry

Mobilizing Men for One-on-One Ministry

MOBILIZING MEN FOR ONE-ON-ONE MINISTRY

STEVE SONDERMAN

BETHANYHOUSE

MINNEAPOLIS, MINNESOTA

Published by Bethany House Publishers
11400 Hampshire Avenue South
Bloomington, Minnesota 55438

Bethany House Publishers is a division of
Baker Publishing Group, Grand Rapids, Michigan.

Printed in the United States of America

Library of Congress Cataloging-in-Publication Data

Sonderman, Steve.
    Mobilizing men for one-on-one ministry : the transforming power of authentic friendship and
discipleship / Steve Sonderman ; foreword by David Murrow.
        p.   cm.
    Summary: "Presents ideas and guidance for meeting the spiritual, emotional, and physical
needs of men through personal ministry. Includes information on how to promote friendships and
discipleship through church-based initiatives. Intended for pastors, layleaders, and individuals"—
Provided by publisher.
    Includes bibliographical references (p.   ).
    ISBN 978-0-7642-0790-7 (pbk. alk. paper)   1. Church work with men.   I. Title.
    BV4440.S665   2010
    259.081—dc22

                                                                                    2010015681

To
John Slack
1955–2006

John introduced me to Jesus and then spent countless hours
discipling me. He lives on in two ways: in eternity with Jesus and
in the hundreds of men he influenced for Jesus.

STEVE SONDERMAN leads the men's ministry at Elmbrook Church in Brookfield, Wisconsin. Founder of the national No Regrets Men's Ministries, he consults widely, training local churches around the world to move their men out of the pews to grow, learn, and serve. Sonderman is a graduate of the University of Wisconsin—Milwaukee (BS) and Bethel Seminary (MDiv). He makes his home in Wisconsin with his wife, Colleen, and their four children.

Steve Sonderman is available to speak at retreats, conferences, and other special events, or to consult with your church or denomination about men's ministry. You can contact him at:

Steve Sonderman
Elmbrook Church
777 South Barker Road
Brookfield, WI 53045
(262) 786–7051
ssonderman@elmbrook.org

Contents

FOREWORD

At the age of forty-six, I made my first pilgrimage to the Holy Land—Lambeau Field in Green Bay, Wisconsin.

I was born in Green Bay. Delivered by the Packers' team doctor, no less. One arm bleeds green, the other gold.

Sadly, my family left Wisconsin when I was just a lad, so I had never been to Lambeau to see the Packers play—until October 7, 2007. Sunday Night Football. Packers vs. Bears. It doesn't get any better than that.

Leading the Pack that night was the legendary Brett Favre. A week earlier, Favre had become the NFL's career leader for touchdown passes. I got to see the old gunslinger fire touchdown number 423 that evening.

During halftime, I began to wonder: How many of those touchdowns would Favre have completed if he'd decided to play the game on his own? What if number 4 walked onto the field without blockers, receivers, coaches, protective gear, and officials? Even with his abundant talent, it's doubtful that Favre would have gained a single yard under those conditions. This future Hall of Famer would have ended up flat on his back (or in the hospital) after one play.

You can't do football on your own. It's hard. It requires coaching. Support. Protection. Goals.

Ministry is like football. It's hard. It requires coaching. Support. Protection. Goals. It cannot be played solo.

Yet in the church, we often send men out to minister solo. We give them a goal (win the world for Jesus), but we provide little coaching, support, or protection. As a result, even enthusiastic, talented men— potential Hall of Famers—end up crushed by the opposition. Some become so discouraged they leave the game.

Steve Sonderman knows this. That's why he's written this book.

There's no one in America more qualified to write on this topic. There are plenty of people talking about discipleship these days, but Steve's been doing it for almost two decades. His church has about fifteen hundred men in discipleship groups at any given time. (I don't know of another church that approaches this figure.) Many of these men are out ministering regularly all over southern Wisconsin.

Even though this book's title is *Mobilizing Men for One-on-One Ministry*, it's not really about individual ministry at all. It's more about building the support team men need so they're not sacked the moment they step onto the field to serve Jesus.

It's funny. There are a few rare individuals in the church who minister quite successfully on their own. Sonderman writes about such a man in chapter 6 of this book. His name is Mike, and he's built a thriving personal ministry to young believers.

Yet for every self-motivated Mike, there are scores, if not hundreds, of men who would begin a personal ministry if only they had the support. In fact, many of these guys tried ministry, got sacked, and gave up.

Men are not spiritual sluggards—they want to get off the bench and into the game. But they don't want to be mangled. They want to score victories for Christ.

Read this book carefully. It will show you how to call, coach, and support men as they compete in the only game that truly matters.

David Murrow
Director, Church for Men

Introduction

W hen I was young, some so-called friends asked me to play hide-and-seek—at midnight, in a just-vacated house. It was pitch black outside, and inside you could only see a couple inches in front of your hand. To make things more interesting, I was the only kid who had never been in the house before. Everyone else knew it front to back. And to make things extra fun, they made me *It* first. Liking a good challenge, I agreed and found a corner to count to a hundred.

After yelling the obligatory "Ready or not, here I come!" I ran for my first victim—and immediately hit a wall and fell in a heap. With my nose bleeding and seeing stars, I slowly pulled myself up and took off again—down an unseen flight of stairs. The fall ended with my head hitting the ground and my wrist feeling like it was broken! I kept at it, but I made so much noise stumbling around that everyone could sneak from room to room. I was *It* the entire time. My night was spent in a state of confusion, not knowing where I was going or what was around the corner.

As I think back on that evening, it reminds me of millions of men today. They are running aimlessly through life in the dark, unable to make sense of the world in which they live. They are hitting walls, stumbling, and causing damage to themselves and others.

There is a reason Jesus calls his followers to be salt and light (Matthew 5:13–16). Not only is he telling us our function in the world, but he is also making a statement about the world itself—that it is full of darkness and like rotting meat. And even though God's light came into the world, Jesus says "men loved darkness" (John 3:19). It was true then and it is true now.

Jesus wants us to see the world the way he does. He wants each of us to encourage the downtrodden, comfort the hurting, provide direction for the wandering, disciple the young, inspire the emerging, welcome the seeking, and share the good news with the lost.

This book is for every man who desires to be an impact player for Christ in his sphere of influence. You and I are surrounded by men who are in need of what only God can provide, and each one of us is in a strategic location to be his hands and feet. He has placed us in just the right church, neighborhood, workplace, and club to have a ministry to the men around us.

Much of what is written today speaks of ministry from the vantage point of what it looks like when done by the church and in the church. It has to do with programmatic-type issues: how to build a successful youth ministry, how to attract and keep new people, how to raise funds for your building campaign, how to lead more effectively, and so on. Little is written to help the ordinary guy in the pew—the guy in the marketplace day in and day out who wants to honor God in his work and influence friends and neighbors for Christ. The way I read it, ministry is first and foremost about relationship, one man walking with another man, encouraging and empowering him in his spiritual journey. And you don't have to go far for one-on-one ministry opportunities. Years ago our then senior pastor Stuart Briscoe said, "Your mission field is the space between your two feet." Men, this book is about helping you see men as God does and then equipping you to minister to them in a personal and powerful way.

In the coming chapters I will share biblical principles I have learned in nearly twenty years of working with men at Elmbrook Church in Milwaukee, Wisconsin, as well as with men from all around the world. The first few chapters will cover what one-on-one ministry looks like and how it can meet men where they are at. We'll then look at specific areas of ministry to men, as well as leading a man to Christ, small groups, ministering to guys in their twenties, and helping men in crisis.

This book can be used in a variety of ways. For pastors and other leaders, it will not only help you in your ministry to the men God has entrusted to you, but it can also be a tool for equipping men to more effectively minister to each other and share the ministry load. I have seen it over and over: The more we invest in people, the wider—and deeper—each church's ministry. My hope is that you will pass along the principles and ideas to guys you see who are faithful, available, and teachable (FAT), and even recommend they read the book. I also wrote this book with men's small groups in mind so they could work through it together and be further equipped as a team for God's work.

My prayer is that God will raise up an army of men wholly committed to him and wholly committed to expanding his kingdom across the street and around the world. My desire is the same as John Wesley's, who said years ago, "Give me one hundred [men] who fear nothing but sin and desire nothing but God, and I care not a straw whether they be clergy or lay; such alone will shake the gates of hell and set up the kingdom of God upon the earth in one generation."

May you and I be that type of man.

Leave No Man Behind

01

On October 3, 1993, more than one hundred U.S. Army Rangers and Delta Force soldiers were dropped by helicopters deep in the capital city of Mogadishu to capture a Somali warlord. Under the country's corrupt regime, hundreds of thousands of Somalis were being starved. The easy-in, easy-out mission was to take no more than an hour, but things went terribly wrong and a large firefight erupted. Still, when two U.S. Black Hawk helicopters were shot down and pilot Michael Durant was captured and taken away, his fellow soldiers would not give up.

In one of the most dramatic scenes in a film about the mission, a helicopter flies over the streets of Mogadishu, and Durant's fellow soldiers speak into a sound system for all in the city to hear: "Mike Durant, we won't leave you behind! Mike Durant, we won't leave you behind!" Not only were these words of encouragement for Durant, but they were also a declaration to the enemy: Durant would be brought home to where he belonged. And eleven days later he was released and reunited with his fellow soldiers.

Millions of men in this country and around the world have been shot down, wounded, and held hostage by the enemy. As followers of Jesus, we are soldiers for Jesus in a very real battle—a battle that is claiming more lives than we know. And we need to develop and live with a leave-no-man-behind attitude.

This mindset may require a paradigm shift in how you and your church minister to men. Much of what we have done in the past was based on events, activities, and programs. They certainly have a place in men's ministry. But ministering to men is not about better and bigger programs; it is about better and stronger relationships.

This book is about how you can have an effective ministry to men in your sphere of influence. No matter your occupation, age, denomination, or ministry training, you have an incredible opportunity to change the course of another man's life.

Through my work leading training seminars and interacting with men over the years, I am convinced that the perfect model for how to minister to men is Jesus. He provides example after example of how to interact with men, teach men, counsel men, challenge men, mobilize men, lead men, and call men to a deeper commitment. Jesus could be called the greatest men's ministry pastor ever, which is why I want to begin with a familiar story from early in his ministry that will give us a vision for ministry to men and the type of man God uses.

The story, found in Mark 2, is of four good friends who learn that Jesus, the miracle worker, is coming to town. They resolve to take their paralyzed friend to Jesus so he can be healed. In my mind, they told him they would pick him up the next morning, probably 9 a.m. sharp, and they literally meant pick him up! Grabbing the corners of his mat, they carry him to the house where Jesus is teaching. The house is packed, though—standing room only—so they take their buddy to the roof, make a hole, and lower him right into the presence of Jesus. Just imagine what the homeowner and guests were thinking as the roof opened up. Just imagine Jesus in the middle of a three-point sermon and it starts to snow thatch.

Why would these friends go to such trouble? Because they knew a man would be changed, healed, and transformed when brought into the presence of God. These ordinary men, most likely with no theological training, believed they could do something extraordinary in the life of their friend if they only got him to Jesus.

It is no different today. God is looking for ordinary men to reach out to the men around them in the name of Jesus.

In this passage from Mark, we see four qualities of a leave-no-man-behind attitude and lifestyle.

1. Men of Commitment

This whole story takes place due to deep male friendships. In today's church world, we would say the four men had an overwhelming commitment to people over buildings, bucks, or programs. They were the friends the man needed to get to Jesus and be healed and forgiven. Just being friends was a big deal back then. The man had two things going against him. First, people with physical deformities were normally ostracized from society and sometimes even disowned, left to fend for themselves. Second, it was thought that people with physical problems must have done something to bring it on themselves. We see this cultural attitude in John 9 when Jesus comes across a man born blind and the disciples ask Jesus, "Who sinned, this man or his parents, that he was born blind?"

The paralyzed man's friends were not going to allow social stigma or physical obstacles to affect their ministry to him. They understood why Jesus came—for people. People who are needy, broken, hurting; the desperate of the world. The friends' commitment to this man was great—their passion for his healing so intense—that they would have done anything to get him to Jesus.

I just love what Alan Redpath says in his wonderful commentary on Nehemiah: "You will never lighten the load until you feel the pressure on your soul."[1] If we are going to have an effective ministry to men, it starts with feeling pressure on your soul, seeing men as Jesus sees them.

We men tend to devote massive amounts of time to making money, enjoying our hobbies, and succeeding at our jobs, yet we often neglect what is most important: people. Seeing men as God does starts with a commitment to looking around and having Holy Spirit sensitivity to the needs of others. Allow me to remind you that every man has a mat, a place of brokenness, a weakness in his life. Every man has a wound that needs healing. Every man has a need for others to carry him at times.

- Men who have lost their jobs
- Men who have lost a spouse or loved one
- Men who struggle with pornography
- Men whose anger is explosive and uncontrolled
- Men who feel like failures
- Men whose marriages are crumbling
- Men whose teenagers are involved in drugs

Look around and you will see men lying on the side of the road just waiting for someone to help them into the presence of Jesus.

The movie *World Trade Center* presents a powerful look at personal commitment. It shows the tragic events of September 11 through the eyes of two U.S. Marines. On their own, they had separately gone to the Twin Towers site to help out. As the story unfolds, the two men meet and find themselves searching through the debris late at night after other rescuers have left. A tapping noise gets their attention and they soon make eye contact with two policemen trapped some forty feet below the surface. When the marines tell them they are going to get help, the policemen plead, "Please, don't leave us." One of the marines answers, "We are the Marines. You are our mission."

Men, we are sons of God. Men are his mission, so they are our mission. In Colossians, Paul wrote, "Devote yourselves to prayer, being *watchful* and thankful" (4:2). May I encourage you to start each day with a rather simple prayer: "Lord, open my eyes to the needs of those around me." As you go through your day, ask God to give you the vision to see the "mats" of men in your sphere of influence.

2. a Commitment to Take Jesus at His Word

Jesus said he came to preach good news to the poor, to proclaim freedom for the prisoners, recovery of sight for the blind, and to release the oppressed (Luke 4:18). The four men believed that Jesus could heal their

3. A Consistent Life

In 1 Thessalonians 2:3, Paul makes a point of telling the church that he came to them with no faulty motives, deceit, or hidden agenda. And in 2:10, he says, "You are witnesses, and so is God, of how holy, righteous and blameless we were among you." Paul is saying loud and clear that there was always consistency between the faith he professed and the life he lived.

Men in your sphere of influence are watching you daily to see if this is true of you. The biggest rap against the church in America today is hypocrisy: people who say one thing and do another. And many surveys do show there is little difference between those who go to church and those who don't. When it comes to ethics, divorce rates, and spending habits, the main difference is where we spend Sunday mornings. That's it!

The story is told of two brothers who owned a construction company. They attended church, sat in the front pew, gave money, and did things to be noticed. But Monday through Saturday they lived the wild life. The new pastor at the church caught on very quickly. When one brother died unexpectedly, the other brother came to the new pastor and said he would give him a check for two million dollars to cover the rest of the church's building program, but there was one condition: At the funeral, the pastor had to say the brother was a saint. This put the pastor in a difficult position. The church needed the money to finish the project, but he did not want to lie. In the end he took the check, put it in the bank, and went to church for the funeral. Standing in front of the gathered, he said, "I want you all to know that this man was a cheat, a swindler, an adulterer, a liar, a hypocrite, and a drunk, but compared to his brother he was a saint!"

Guys: Just like the pastor, the men around you can spot a phony. If we are going to be effective, Paul says we must live an authentic life. We must reflect in our lives the message we speak with our lips. Is there congruency between what you say on Sunday morning and how you live during the week? People want to see if God is real, if you're authentic, and if he makes any difference in the way you live your life.

Robert Murray McCheyne, the great Scottish preacher, once said,

"The greatest need of my people is my personal holiness."[4] Men, the greatest gift you will give your wife, your children, your work associates, your small group, and your neighbors is your personal holiness. Our lives are to point to Jesus. As a minister of Jesus Christ, you will be no more effective than the life you live. Your manner of living prepares the way for the reception of your words.

4. Genuine Love

Another key quality of one-on-one ministry is genuine love. In 1 Thessalonians 2:7, Paul writes, "We were gentle among you, like a mother caring for her little children." I find it interesting that this tough, masculine apostle makes his point using a feminine metaphor, a picture of a young mom holding a baby close to her breast, imparting life to the child. In the next verse he says, "We loved you so much." In verses 11–12 he writes, "We dealt with each of you as a father . . . encouraging, comforting and urging you." Paul's ministry was definitely marked by love, just as the ministry of Jesus was.

Jesus loved rich people and poor people, old people and young people, educated and uneducated, the sick and the healthy. In all he did and taught, he demonstrated a love for people.

Facing death on the cross, his love for his mother came through. His love for the soldiers was seen in his forgiving them. At the end of his life, his love for the thief was evident. No one in all of history has demonstrated a love for people as we see in Jesus. In Jesus we see a radical inclusivity and acceptance of people. It is this unconditional love that melts even the hardest heart and draws it to the Father's heart.

Men, we live in a love-starved society. And as the song says, people are looking for love in all the wrong places. Jesus says, if you want to leave your mark on a person or society, if you want to start a cultural revolution, if you want heads to turn and take notice, it will begin and end with LOVE. It will be an unconditional, self-sacrificing, all-inclusive, irrational acceptance of people.

What would happen if we were radically inclusive with the people we met during the course of our day? If we really believed that as ministers of Jesus Christ in the schools, neighborhoods, and workplaces, that our fundamental job is to love people, no matter who they are—lost, found, rich, poor, young, old, black, or white.

I will never forget a sophomore who came to the high school Bible study I led while I was in college. Tom came with his older brother, sat in the back, ate the food, and watched from a distance. Gradually he got more and more involved, and by his senior year he was one of the leaders in the ministry. One day I took Tom to breakfast and asked him to tell me his story. He said at first he didn't want to come to the Bible study, but his older brother dragged him. It wasn't so bad, though, meeting some nice girls and eating the great snacks. Plus, it was a good reason not to do his homework! But what really impacted Tom was the seniors. They would talk to him in the halls at school and on the football field, and on weekends they'd call him and invite him to do things. He said it was their love that drew him to Christ. If I am not mistaken, that sounds a lot like John 13:35, where Jesus says, "Men will know that you are my disciples, if you love one another." Tom is now serving as a Jesuit priest out West and reflects the love of Christ to others.

One-on-one ministry to a man will be marked by a motherly type of love that is caring and tender when he loses his job, his marriage is in jeopardy, or his health endangered. But there will be times when a fatherly type of love will be needed as well—a tough love, a love that confronts and challenges. Whatever the case, we are to be a conduit of the love of Jesus to the world.

5. Use the Word

Paul says in 1 Thessalonians 2:13, "We also thank God continually because, when you received the word of God, which you heard from us, you accepted it not as the word of men, but as it actually is, the word of God, which is at work in you." What an incredible verse. To work with men, the Lord has given us the greatest tool: the Bible. The Bible reveals God's purpose for our lives, promises to live by, and principles to order our lives by. To merely accept it intellectually won't change a person, but when we welcome it into our lives and act on it and obey it, we will be permanently changed. Jesus certainly lived by God's Word. He quoted the Old Testament ninety times from seventy different chapters.

I love the passage in 2 Timothy 2:15 where Paul says we are to be workmen who correctly handle the word of truth. I have this picture in my mind of a person going off to work, and in his life toolbox is the Word of God to:

- comfort a sick friend, a grieving friend, a friend who is going through a relationship breakup.

- encourage a friend or work associate who needs a word to pick them up.

- teach kingdom values and principles to children or fellow members in a small group.

- guide people in making the right decisions based on principles from Scripture.

One of my best memories is attending Fellowship of Christian Athletes meetings every Sunday afternoon during high school. I especially remember a particular guest speaker, John Slack. As he talked about God's love for us, he was constantly quoting Scriptures and referring to the Bible. I was seated next to him, and I noticed his Bible was all marked up with underlined passages and notes everywhere. I had never seen anything like that before. So after the meeting I asked if we could get together and talk. He invited me and a few other guys to start a Bible study of Genesis. We spent hours and hours reading and asking questions, and for the first time I was actually excited about the Bible and what it had to say. Over time my life began to change; a Christian worldview was developing in my heart, I was acquiring new principles for living, and I was being transformed. I was not only being trained to study but was also equipped to impart it to others. I can honestly say my desire for reading, studying, and teaching the Word started back in that initial small group with John, whose only tool was the Bible.

I hope now you understand the reason that I absolutely love 1 Thessalonians 2:1–13 and why I wanted to share these principles. They lay a wonderful foundation for one-on-one ministry, and they are principles we will return to over and over again. Nowhere in this passage does Paul talk about a ministry event or activity, nor does he talk about brochures or table decorations. Rather, Paul simply shares his heart and the deep love he has for the Thessalonians, a love that stems from the personal relationships he developed over time. It will be no different for us.

NOTES

1. Stephen Covey, *The 7 Habits of Highly Effective People* (New York: Simon & Schuster, 1989), 98.

2. Greg Ogden, *Transforming Discipleship* (Downers Grove, IL: Inter-Varsity Press, 2003), 69.

3. E. M. Bounds, *The Complete Works of Prayer by E. M. Bounds* (Grand Rapids, MI: Baker Books, 1990), 550–551.

4. Quote by Robert Murray McCheyne, http://web.ukonline.co.uk/d .haslam/mccheyne/rmmquotes.htm.

What in the World Do Men Want in Life?

03

We men are known for leaving a lot of things unsaid. It can take a while before we let our guard down with other guys, which is why personal ministry is so important. In a one-on-one situation or small group, you can really find out where a guy's at in life.

There are some issues, though, that men rarely talk about but greatly impact how we should approach ministry, especially if we are trying to mobilize a group of men. I have learned over the years that certain inner needs—what men want in life—carry over to how they view church and respond to ministry.

David Letterman's Top Ten lists are famous. Here I offer my own list of what men want in life today, plus ministry application points. Unlike Dave, however, I don't claim my list is in order. I think each point is vitally important. Nevertheless, I give you *The Top Ten Things Men Want in Life!*

1. *Men are looking for relevance.* Many men do not see the value in going to church because it is not speaking their language or addressing the issues men are facing. Most surveys tell us that close to two-thirds of men do not attend church because they view it as irrelevant to them. For example, recently I saw a survey say that 92 percent of churchgoing men had never heard a sermon on the subject of work. This implies that what you do for forty to seventy hours a week does not relate to what happens in church on Sunday morning. The message is, church is

irrelevant. Many churches today are very good at answering questions men are not asking, but they are not answering the questions men are asking!

The top issues for men are work, family, marriage, sexuality, and finances, and rarely are these addressed in the church today.

Application: If you are a small-group leader, make sure you are studying issues relevant to men. If you find yourself in a teaching or preaching situation, be sure to address men-related issues. When conversing with men at work or in the neighborhood, steer conversations to core interests of men.

Here are questions men are asking today:

- What is true masculinity?

- What is success?

- How do I deal with feelings of guilt?

- What is male sexuality? Is purity possible today?

- What does a healthy marriage look like?

- How can I raise my children to be successful in the eyes of God?

- How can I be a man of integrity in the workplace?

- How can I survive an economic meltdown?

- How can I be a leader in the home, church, and workplace?

- What is my purpose in life?

2. *Men want to be involved in a cause greater than themselves.* Men are looking for a compelling vision. When Steve Jobs of Apple put together his original team of engineers, he issued this challenge: "I want to put a ding in the universe." And boy, has Apple ever dinged the universe! Men today want to be about the work of the kingdom and its expansion. They want to know what hill you are climbing and where you are going. Men are not going to give their time, money, and energy to move

papers around and attend committee meetings. They want to know, "Am I going to make a difference in the world?"

Application: In our interactions with men, we need to continually put the vision before them that they are a part of something much bigger than themselves. We need to restate the vision of the church and ministry on a regular basis. God has given us the greatest vision humanity can have. With heaven and hell hanging in the balance, men have the opportunity to impact a person's eternity. Read what Bill Hybels of Willow Creek says about the potential of the church and our involvement in it:

"There is nothing like the local church when it's working right. Its beauty is indescribable. Its power is breathtaking. Its potential is unlimited. It comforts the grieving and heals the broken. . . . It builds bridges to seekers and offers truth to the confused. It provides resources for those in need and opens its arms to the forgotten, the downtrodden, and the disillusioned. It breaks the chains of addictions, frees the oppressed, and offers belonging to the marginalized of this world. Whatever the capacity for human suffering the church has a greater capacity for healing and wholeness. . . . No other organization on earth is like the church, nothing even comes close."[1] Who wouldn't want to be a part of something like this? We cannot hold this back.

A second application is to do ministry in teams because men love to be a part of a team. This goes back to their days of junior high and high school. Whenever I am helping a man find his place of service in the church, I try to connect him with others he can serve with. This sense of belonging and team spirit make it much easier for him to get started.

A final application is to give your men a variety of ministry opportunities that will stretch them and expose them to the needs of the world. They need to see the church worldwide and all God is doing. For example, to help men grasp the tremendous growth of the church in the Southern Hemisphere and how it is sending the most missionaries to the world, we can organize trips for medical care workers to the Philippines, tradesmen to build homes in Guatemala, or everyday guys to help earthquake cleanup in Haiti. It makes a big impact when men see they are a part of something much bigger than themselves.

3. *Men want a shot at greatness.* I don't know about you, but I have

never met a man who wanted to be a failure or a loser. Men want to win. They want to be a hero. Most churches today want nice men, not great men. But men are looking for significance, asking, "Why am I here and what difference does it make?" One of the greatest fears men have is the fear of failure. And this fear will drive them in so many ways, some healthy and some unhealthy. We have to help them through this.

When I fly, I often strike up conversations with the person next to me by asking their name and what they do. After talking for a while, sometimes too long, they will ask me what I do. From experience, I know that if I tell them I am a pastor right away, the conversation will quickly end. So I've learned to say, "My job is to empower men to be champions in life." Of course, this gets most people interested and asking questions, which normally leads to a significant conversation. In some ways this is a job description for each of us, whether we are a pastor, layleader, or everyday guy: We are to empower men to be champions in life. Let me share some practical ways you can do that.

Application: First, men need to be encouraged. They are usually beat up all day long and they need a cheerleader. Very few of your men have a boss waiting at the front door of their workplace thanking them for coming to work and thanking them for the vital contribution they are making to the company. My guess is that none of your guys have children who are waiting on the driveway when they come home from work, wanting to thank them for working ten hours that day so they can have a roof over their heads and food on the table! When they turn on the TV at night, they are beat up again as the average sitcom makes men out to be idiots. One of the greatest gifts you can give your men is encouragement. When they take a step of faith, when they say no to sin, when they give time to serve, encourage them; let them know you are in their corner.

A second application is to help men catch a vision for what they can become, and then release them to pursue that vision. Most men in our society do not have a compelling vision of manhood, a vision that calls them up as men. Most men do not know what God's purposes for their life are, and they are simply going through life trying to survive. In one-on-one conversations and small groups, don't miss the opportunity to share what it means to be a man and how God wants to work out his purposes in and through their lives.

4. *Men want to be challenged.* Before starting our church's ministry to men, I surveyed our men and heard over and over, "I want to be challenged." Men grow up with challenges. In school it's the big exam. In athletics it's the big game. In the business world it's the big sale, a new product, or a new venture.

When it comes to faith, we make it too easy on men. We expect too little. When I read the Gospels, I see Jesus over and over again drawing a line in the sand and daring the disciples to meet him on his side. It's no different today. Men want to be challenged to act, pray, and think in a way that glorifies God. I find it helpful to remind the men often what is at stake—that we are dealing with kingdom realities. Each of us can help change a person's eternal destiny, and God has given us the privilege to join him in what he is doing around the world.

Men tend to view everything around them as something to be overcome or conquered. Take shopping, for example. For most women, shopping is an experience. My wife and daughters can get up in the morning, go get their coffee, then spend the entire day at the mall and come back with nothing and say it was the best day of their lives! If they actually buy something, which they normally do, it is like nirvana! Most men see shopping as a challenge. They are thinking, *How fast can I find it, buy it, and get it home?* No wonder so many men do their Christmas shopping on Christmas Eve—because it is a challenge to get it done in the shortest amount of time.

I can tell you right now, men are sick and tired of not being challenged. They don't want to check their competitive drive at the door of the church. Rather than talk about sports, the weather, or the stock market, they are looking for risk, adventure, change, competition, and expansion.

Application: First, raise the standards of what is expected. Challenge men to give more, to take a missions trip, to lead a small group, to serve in a city ministry. It will be different for every man you are working with, but the bottom line is to personally challenge them to take the next step in their development. Since the beginning of our ministry, we have asked men to join our thirty-two-week Basic Training Discipleship course, which involves two hours in class and two hours out of class each week. When we started this class, people told us we were crazy. Men don't like to read, they said . . . or memorize Scripture, or share and be accountable. Well, say what you want, but almost one thousand men have gone through that course and are leading all over the church! Men want to be challenged. Don't lower the bar; instead, raise the bar on what you expect from your men.

5. *Men are looking for action.* Men today are looking for something to do. They do not like sitting around. Men measure themselves by what they do, what they accomplish, or what they get done with their hands. Their goal orientation pushes them to achieve things, to focus until the task is accomplished. I have found that men enjoy working on projects where the results are solid and tangible. Men are drawn toward action-oriented activities rather than those more sedentary in nature. What we have discovered over the years is that side-by-side experience often turns to face-to-face. Men want to be on the offensive, not the defensive. Unfortunately, most churches today are in maintenance mode and not missional mode. Most have settled for rearranging the chairs on the deck while the ship is going down. We need to ask men to get into the game and then give them something to do.

Application: The first application is to build into your ministry opportunities for men to serve outside the church—projects like Habitat for Humanity, helping at a rescue mission, and tutoring students. An excellent book on the subject is *The Externally Focused Church*. We have seen so many men from the community get involved in service projects and work teams because there is something in each of us that wants to contribute to and improve our community. In the midst of this, we need to be patient, as it can take a long time for a man to move from service to commitment to Christ.

A second application is to provide opportunities for your men to discover their spiritual gifts and then deploy them. Put together a spiritual gifts class so men can discover how God wired them. They'll discover their optimal place of service. You can also offer to take your men through a study to help them in this area. A couple of helpful books are

Holy Discontent by Bill Hybels and *S.H.A.P.E.: Finding and Fulfilling Your Unique Purpose for Life* by Erik Rees.

6. *Men are looking for leaders and want to become leaders.* Men do not follow programs, they follow men. They are looking for strong, masculine leadership, and the church needs to provide it if we want men to become a part of the church. They want to follow a bold, courageous visionary leader. If you are a pastor, a small-group leader, or a men's ministry leader, then lead. If you lead, they will follow. But not only are they looking for a leader to follow, they want to become a leader themselves. They want to lead in their family, workplace, church, community, and world. Oftentimes they do not know how and they are looking to the church for training. The question we have to continually ask is, "What can we do to help them become the leader they want to be?"

Application: In everything you do, make sure you are modeling and teaching the basics of leadership. A leadership study could be done on the character of a leader, the calling of a leader, and the competencies of a leader. Some great books I have used in the past are *Leadership Essentials* by Greg Ogden, *Spiritual Leadership* by Henry Blackaby, and *Courageous Leadership* by Bill Hybels. Leadership equipping has to be hands-on as well. For example, if you are talking to your men about being the spiritual leader in their homes, be sure not to give them a guilt trip, but provide some very practical teaching and examples of what it looks like. Explain to them how they can read the Bible to their kids before they go to bed and model prayer alongside their wife, and give them examples of how they can serve as a family.

7. *Men are looking to have fun.* When most men walk into a church, they see a bunch of serious, stoic, or even sad-looking people. Men love to laugh and have fun. They love a great joke, funny story, or good movie. For most men life is already very hard, very serious, and just plain work. Very few men have an outlet where they can be themselves, joke around, and laugh a little. I would encourage you to build into your ministry to men the opportunity for them to have fun, whether it is going to a game together, hunting, fishing, or having a movie night. There are many things you can do with men to allow them to unwind a bit, relax, and have some fun. Everything does not always have to be so serious.

Application: There are a number of things you can do to bring fun into your relationships and ministry to men. You can plan some activities that may not have any deep spiritual significance. For example, have a game night at your house, invite some guys over to watch a ball game, go to a game together, go hunting or fishing, go canoeing, or play golf together. All of these activities get a man out of his normal routine and allow him the opportunity to unwind. During some of your large-group gatherings, show some blooper videos or use jokes and funny stories as part of your program or message. Whenever possible, give men a chance to laugh and enjoy themselves.

8. *Men are looking for brothers.* Men have something within them that wants to have a friend, but they don't know how. Part of being made in the likeness of God is to be made for relationship with others, yet we struggle with it. Most men today have many acquaintances but few deep friendships. They have buddies to play golf with but not anyone they can call at two in the morning when their wife leaves them. Most men do not have models of what healthy male friendships look like, much less how to develop one. There is the underlying fear of being considered homosexual if they are in a deep relationship with another man.

Application: There are a few things you can do to help the men in your sphere of influence. First, teach about relationships on a regular basis in your small groups, on Sunday mornings, etc. Second, model it for the men of your church. They will learn the most by watching you model relationships. As you build solid, authentic friendships with others, they will watch and learn. The final thing you can do is provide an environment where men can build healthy male friendships. For example, if you have a gathering of men for any occasion, allow plenty of time for them to mill around and talk with one another, or allow discussion time after the talk at your breakfast gathering. You do not always have to keep them busy the whole time they are at the activity.

9. *Men are looking for healing.* Men are carrying around a bag of wounds, hurts, and brokenness that needs to be healed. I would go so far as to say that every man has a wound of one sort or another, and sometimes they do not realize it. For most, they are the walking wounded

of society. They have father, mother, work, or divorce wounds that are creating havoc in their lives and the lives of those around them. Many try to anesthetize their pain with sex, drugs, or alcohol. If we are going to have an effective ministry to the men of our church, we have to provide a place where they can experience healing in their lives. There will need to be a person or place they can go to that is safe.

Application: One of the most important things you can do is provide a small group where men will feel free to share their wounds and deal with them. The group leader or leaders need to be trained on how to develop a safe environment where men feel they can be vulnerable and transparent with all they are going through. (I will discuss this more in chapter 10.) One of the best resources today is the material Robert Lewis developed as part of Men's Fraternity Bible study. The first year, *The Quest for Authentic Manhood*, looks specifically at various wounds men have and how to bring healing to them.

A second application will be in your one-on-one talks with men. Oftentimes when I am meeting with men, I ask how they have been hurt in the past. They usually give me this look that says, *What in the world do you mean?* At this time I can share the different types of wounds men are dealing with today, plus my own wounds and how they have been healed. It doesn't take long for a man to open up and start sharing about his own life and woundedness.

10. *Men want to be spoken to in their language.* Much of the language we use in the church today is more feminine in nature. We use terms like *sharing, relationship, saved, intimacy with Jesus,* and *fellowship.* When I first started working with the men of our church, I wrote a newsletter and, before sending it, gave it to a friend to check my language. I asked him to circle any words or phrases that were feminine in nature. The newsletter came back completely red! Over the years I have learned to speak male, and you can too.

Application: With your leadership team or a few other guys, have a brainstorming session on what words men gravitate toward. A few examples are *adventure, risk, challenge, leadership, game plan, team, victory, win, success, build, partnership,* and *dangerous.* Use this type of language in any newsletters you produce, or brochures, event flyers, or announcements in the bulletin. If you are preaching or teaching, use stories men can relate to and provide stories with plenty of application.

As I look back on this Top Ten list, I can see how it might be overwhelming. But these inner needs of men can also be exciting and empowering for ministry purposes. Before moving on, I would encourage you to work through the following exercise individually or with your ministry team.

Exercise—What Do Men Want in Life?

Take each of the ten lessons learned about men and discuss how they impact how you design your ministry to the men in your sphere of influence.

1. Men are looking for relevance.
    What are the questions men are asking today?

    How can you/we address these in our ministry plan?

2. Men want to be involved in a cause greater than themselves.
    How is this manifested in men?

    How can you share the vision of your church and ministry with your men?

    How can you help your men catch that vision and own it?

3. Men want a shot at greatness.
    How is this manifested in men?

What does it mean for you to empower men to be champions in life?

How can you practically encourage other men on a regular basis?

4. Men want to be challenged.
   How have we lowered the bar in the church today?

   What does making the "big ask" look like for you?

5. Men are looking for action.
   How is this manifested in men?

   What are some ways you can get your men out of their comfort zone?

   How can you help men discover their spiritual gifts?

6. Men are looking for leaders and want to become leaders.
   Where do you have to grow in your leadership skills?

   What is your plan for growing leaders?

7. Men are looking to have fun.
   How is this manifested in men?

What can you do to incorporate a little fun into your ministry to men?

8. Men are looking for brothers.
   Why do men struggle in this area so much?

   How can you help men develop friendships with one another?

9. Men are looking for healing.
   How is this manifested in men?

   What can you do to help men heal?

10. Men want to be spoken to in their language.
    What are some examples of feminine language we use in the church?

    What are some words or phrases that will resonate with guys?

NOTES

1. Bill Hybels, *Courageous Leadership* (Grand Rapids, MI: Zondervan, 2002), 23.

04

Nate was in his mid-twenties when I performed his marriage ceremony. Soon after, I invited him to a class on authentic manhood that I taught on Wednesday mornings. We would get together once in a while to talk and go over any questions he had. Then, right before Christmas, I shared the true meaning of Christmas with him. Nate went home and gave his heart to Jesus.

Jim, in his thirties, was invited by a friend to go on a missions trip to help cleanup efforts after Hurricane Katrina. During the twenty-hour van ride, Jim was quiet and listened to the conversations. Upon the team's arrival, he watched and listened for the first few days. Finally he could not stand it any longer and started to ask questions about why people on the team were "different" from most people he knew. That week Jim gave control of his life to Jesus.

In October 2008, Bob joined the thousands of others who had lost their jobs due to the bad economy. He heard about our weekly career counseling meetings, and after a few weeks he realized his greatest need was not a job but a Savior, and he gave his life to Jesus.

Mark and his wife had been attending Elmbrook for about fifteen years, and during that time they sat under some incredible Bible teaching. After hearing the Word of God being preached for all those years and never responding, Mark was finally able to yield the leadership of his life to Jesus.

Mike had gone to church his entire life. He knew Bible stories and could recite Scriptures, but as an athlete he just did not think it was cool for a man to be a sold-out Christian. A co-worker invited him to our annual No Regrets Men's Conference. When Mike walked into the sanctuary, he saw over three thousand men worshiping at the top of their lungs. It was not the words that drew him to Christ but the worship and being in the presence of God that did!

For the sake of time and space, I will stop the stories here, but I could go on and on. There is absolutely nothing more exciting and rewarding than to see a man who has been living without Jesus finally surrender his life to him. What I have seen over the years—and I hope these stories reflect this—is that God uses a variety of ways to draw men to himself.

This chapter focuses on principles and ideas for pointing a man to Christ. Each of us knows men who have not given their lives to Christ. And this information will help equip you and the guys in your church to be effective witnesses for him.

Principle #1: God Uses Ordinary People to Accomplish His Eternal Purposes

We see "ordinary" throughout the Bible. When God wanted to create something as complex as mankind, he chose to use dust. When he wanted to communicate with Moses, he did not send an e-mail, text him, or use satellite communication. He used an ordinary bush—ablaze! When David took on Goliath, he did not use an MX missile, a smart bomb, a tank, or a Black Hawk helicopter, but rather a stone. Jesus was not born in a nice hospital or at the Hyatt, but likely in a cave. When Jesus wanted to start a worldwide movement, he chose twelve ordinary men with less-than-impressive résumés.

God loves using the ordinary to do the extraordinary. I grew up reading and listening to Major Ian Thomas of the Torchbearers, and one of his favorite sayings was, "It is not your ability that matters, but your availability." God is not interested in your credentials, education, ability, or age. It is your availability and attitude that matter most to him.

You may be deathly afraid of the "E" word: evangelism. You may be unsure what to say or when to say it. You may be afraid that if you do not "close the deal" there is something wrong with you. Men, I want to tell you right from the start that no matter how long you have been a follower of Jesus, how much training you have had, or what fears you have, God wants to use you to reach other men. He is not going to make you do anything goofy or weird. Just be the person God made you to be, be available to him, and watch out.

May I challenge you to wake up in the morning and pray a dangerous prayer? "God, thank you for this day. I surrender myself to you and am available to you to be used by you in any way you desire." I can tell you that if you pray this prayer, God is going to bring more people into your life than you will know what to do with.

Principle #2: It Starts With Prayer

One of my favorite quotes by E. M. Bounds is, "Talking to men for God is a great thing, but talking to God for men is greater still."[1] If we are going to see men's lives changed, it starts with prayer. The walls around the hearts of men are too high and too thick to think that we can get rid of them through our own ingenuity and know-how. One passage that has been extremely helpful in my prayer life as it regards to evangelism is Colossians 4:2–6:

> Devote yourselves to prayer, being watchful and thankful. And pray for us, too, that God may open a door for our message, so that we may proclaim the mystery of Christ, for which I am in chains. Pray that I may proclaim it clearly, as I should. Be wise in the way you act toward outsiders; make the most of every opportunity. Let your conversation be always full of grace, seasoned with salt, so that you may know how to answer everyone.

Prayer is to be a regular part of our life—not an add-on or something we do if we feel like it. Paul says we are to be "watchful," which brings with it the idea of keeping our eyes open to the needs of others, and looking for open doors and opportunities to serve, encourage, and listen. It is interesting that Paul prays for "open doors." Being under house arrest, he is not praying for the prison doors to fly open but rather that in the midst of his difficult situation, he would have opportunities to speak of Christ. He prays for effective ministry in the place God has put him. So what open doors do you see? With your neighbors? With your co-workers? With your family? With your friends?

Paul continues by asking that he would proclaim the message clearly. He also puts importance on wise actions toward others. In a sense he is saying there should be consistency between what our lips say on Sunday and how we live during the week. Each of us has to ask the Holy Spirit to shine the light of his holiness into our lives so there is not an area in our life that cancels the impact of our spoken testimony. Finally, Paul talks about speech being full of grace and seasoned with salt. He understands the power of words.

I want to encourage you to write this passage on a note card and make it your prayer every morning when you wake up.

Application: Take time to list a few men in your sphere of influence and a need you have seen in their life. How can you help meet the need?

Person: _____

Need: _____

Person: _____

Need: _____

Person: _____

Need: _____

Person: _____

Need: _____

Principle #3: Evangelism Is a Process, Not a Religious Activity

Evangelism is a process, not a Tuesday night mugging session. Many people have grown up with a model of evangelism where it is strictly an activity to do or a notch to add to your belt. But the true picture of evangelism in Scripture, especially in the Gospels, is that of farming. When we look at John 4:25–38, we discover three aspects to the process. The first is cultivating. This is the intentional building of relationships with those who are far from the faith. Through these relationships they will see Christ in you, experience the love of Christ through you, and hopefully any false caricatures they may have regarding Christianity can be broken down. Second, pointing a man to Christ involves planting, often interjecting faith statements and ideas into the relationship by asking questions, answering questions, and sharing your story. Finally there is reaping, which is making a clear presentation of the gospel and allowing the person to respond.

I have found that seeing evangelism as a process takes the pressure off. In my early days I was led to believe that unless the person prayed the sinner's prayer, I was a failure. Now I realize I am just one of many links in the chain. For example, a few years ago my wife, Colleen, and I went out with a couple we knew from the youth basketball team I coached. At one point in our conversation, the man said, "Steve, I am just not as religious as you." My response was, "Bill, I am not religious. Matter of fact, I gave up on religion when I was eighteen. I discovered then that religion was man trying to earn God's favor and that Christianity was Christ doing for me what I could not do myself." There wasn't an opening to say much more about faith. I did not share the four spiritual laws or show him the bridge diagram (page 61) for how a person can get to God. But I know I was involved in the process of watering seeds that had been planted and perhaps helped him see the truth of the gospel.

Dan Spader, in his exhaustive work with high school ministry and evangelism, has discovered that the typical unchurched person must get to know at least 5.3 believers relationally before they will trust the message of Christ, and they must hear the message five to seven times before they fully understand it.[2] This is why we should see evangelism as a process, not an activity. People today are so far from the cross of

Christ it can take months, even years, for a person to fully understand the gospel and commit their life to Christ.

Principle #4: We Must Leave Our Comfort Zone

In Matthew 5:13–16, Jesus uses the element of salt to describe to the disciples how they are to make an impact in the world. The disciples might have pictured fishermen rubbing salt into their catch to preserve it for the journey to market. For the salt to work, it had to go deep.

The church in the book of Acts penetrated the community, going person to person, village to village, and city to city to share the good news. It never occurred to the early church to sit in the temple and wait for people to come to them, and it is no different today. If we are going to be effective in sharing the good news of Jesus, we must go to the men and not expect them to come to us. We have to leave our comfort zones, our "holy huddles," and go to where the men are living out their lives. I love what George MacLeod, founder of the Iona Community in Scotland, said years ago: "I simply argue that the cross be raised again at the center of the marketplace, as well as on the steeple of the church. I am recovering the claim that Jesus was not crucified in a cathedral between two candles, but on a cross between two thieves; on the town garbage heap; at a crossroad so cosmopolitan that they had to write his title in Hebrew, in Latin, and Greek . . . at the kind of place where cynics talk smut, and thieves curse, and soldiers gamble. Because that's where He died. And that is what He died about. And that is where churchmen ought to be and what churchmen should be about."[3]

So what is the application for each one of us? Early on I found it easy to get so caught up with church work and church people that I could go days, weeks, or even months not even having contact with men who do not know Jesus. That is why years ago I started coaching my children's sports teams. I took my natural love and abilities and used them to engage with men. Those fifteen years of coaching were some of the best times for me to interact with parents and be salt and light. These days I am usually at the gym three days a week, which gives me plenty of opportunities to talk with men who are on the treadmill or stationary bike next to me. Maybe you want to do some coaching, serve on the school board, help out at the school, join a hunting or fishing club, or sign up for a golf league. Your family could have a block party or a game night to get to know your neighbors, or go caroling at Christmas. The bottom line is, men are not going to come to you or to the church; you are going to have to go to them.

Exercise

What has been your normal response to the culture in which you live? Has it been to: isolate from the culture? Assimilate with the culture? Or, engage the culture?

What are some things you enjoy doing that you could do with other men?

What are some things you could do as a family to get to know your neighbors better?

Principle #5: Relationship Building Is Key

In every survey I've seen on how people come to faith, the numbers are always the same. Eighty-five to 90 percent of people come to faith through a friend, family member, or relative. The other 10 percent is through a pastor, evangelistic crusade, radio or TV broadcast, Sunday school class, or church program. It is all about relationship. Unfortunately, if you are like me, you might be relationally challenged, and this whole idea of relationship building can be foreign. Allow me to share a few ideas with you to help in this area:

Live a consistent lifestyle. I've said it before, but the life we live will provide the context and framework for the words we share. I once heard Joe Aldrich say at a pastors conference at Multnomah, "We are to be the good news before you share the good news." Someone else said it something like this: The visualization of the gospel provides the context for the verbalization of the gospel. Cynicism runs deep in the world, and what people are looking for is the real deal. People who will be authentic, real, honest, and genuine. In the movie *Jerry Maguire*, sports agent Jerry gets in a heated conversation with his client. The player famously yells, "Jerry, show me the money! Show me the money!" Our society today is yelling at the church, "Show me your life! Show me your life!" Each of us has to ask God where we are being inconsistent or hypocritical in our lifestyle.

Initiate. Relationships do not just happen. Men are not going to walk up to your front door and ask you to do something. You are going to have to take the initiative to invite them to lunch, to a game, or to a barbecue.

Build relationships with those who accept your social advances. God is not asking you to go find the most difficult person you know and try to be their friend! There are people in your sphere of influence where there is already some affinity. Start there.

Learn to ask questions. One of the great skills in relationship building is the ability to ask questions. Too often we just want to talk about ourselves. I can still remember hearing Becky Pippert at a missions conference years ago saying that evangelism was 50 percent investigative (asking questions), 40 percent stimulating a person's curiosity, and 10 percent relating the message. Asking questions is like unpeeling an onion one layer at a time. By asking questions you are going into the relationship as a learner, not one who has everything figured out. Start with those things that are basic, on the fact level, and then slowly move to interests, values, attitudes, and worldview. As you ask questions you will begin to get a sense of their worldview and how they hold life together.

Accept them for who they are. Do not expect regenerate behavior from unregenerate men. If you go to games, dinner, hunting, or fishing with guys, they are going to do and say things you may not approve of or do yourself. Their behavior is not the issue, their hearts are. You'll probably have to learn to put up with a little foul language or crude humor if you are going to build a relationship with them. Remember that Jesus left the splendor and majesty of heaven to live among us; just think of what he was willing to put up with so that we might have life.

Be creative in what you do. Think and pray through what might be some shared experiences you could have with men in your sphere of influence. What are some ways to open up your home or use various holidays to invite families over?

Be honest with your life. Men will not be impressed that you have your life all together and that you never have any problems. Share your hurts, joys, struggles, fears, and frustrations with them and let them see that just because you are a follower of Jesus, life is not a rose garden. What is different is that you have a God who promises to be with you in the midst of it.

Time, time, time. Guys, I will tell you right now this is not easy, nor is it fast. I am still praying for and building relationships with guys I knew from high school (over thirty years ago). In the same way a farmer cannot pull his crops up to check the roots, we cannot hurry the process. It is God who draws a man to himself, and we need to be patient.

Principle #6: Love and Serve Them

Other than prayer, the greatest weapon we have to see men come to Christ is love. In Matthew 5:16, Jesus tells the disciples to "let your light shine before men, that they may see your good deeds and praise your Father in heaven." And in John 13:35, he says, "All men will know that you are my disciples, if you love one another." Notice he does not say you will be known by the lapel pin on your sport coat, or by the bumper sticker on your car, or by the music you play in your office. The mark of a Christian is love. It was love that softened the hard heart of a soldier at the foot of the cross. When the soldier saw Jesus hanging, bleeding, and dying for the world, he said, "This truly was the Son of God." Like the Good Samaritan walking down the road, we must have our eyes open to see the needs of those around us. I will tell you right now there are men in the ditch everywhere who need some good old-fashioned love and care.

Principle #7: Look for Open Doors

Everyone sees the gospel through a different window. When Jesus walked this earth, he constantly presented himself in new and different ways because he knew that every person would see God in different ways. For example, for those who are lonely, Jesus is a place to belong; for those with a fear of death, he provides eternal life; for those with relationship problems, he is the reconciler; for those with a low self-esteem, he says you matter to God; for those ridden with guilt, he says he will forgive you; for those who lack direction in life, he will give you a sense of purpose.

One of the great joys I have had in the last few years is teaching at pastors' conferences with my good friend Kenny Luck, the men's ministry pastor at Saddleback Church and founder of Everyman Ministries. In his teaching on ministering to men, he says there are four streams by which men are coming to Christ, and I have found the same to be true in our ministry to men.

- *Through a need.* We've talked about it before, but men today are wounded and hurt in a number of different ways. Whether addicted to alcohol, drugs, work, or pornography, or going through unemployment or the loss of a wife or child, men in these very difficult places are very open to the gospel. This gives you individually and as a church an excellent opportunity to introduce Christ to them.

- *Through having fun.* With all the stresses of life, men are looking for a way to relax and have fun. Just this weekend our Outdoors Ministry had a sport clay shooting day, and men had the opportunity to bring their friends and shoot guns together. It was exciting because there were many new men there. You can have fun in so many healthy ways, and I'd encourage you to explore different avenues for you and your friends to spend time together.

- *Through a cause.* Men want to make a difference. I have found that it is easy to invite a man to help with a cleanup project, serve food, tutor, help after a natural disaster, or some other way to improve the community. Meeting community needs is a wonderful way for a man to take the first step toward Christ.

- *Through a relationship.* This is why this book exists. I am continually encouraging our men to stop some of their church activities so they have time to build relationships. We know that generally within two years of becoming a Christian most people no longer have any relationships with unchurched people. The reason, of course, is they get so involved at church and busy with church activities they have no time for those outside the church. You will need to declare war on busyness if you are to break the trend.

Principle #8: Share Your Story

Stories are a powerful means of communication. Politicians understand this, advertisers understand this, and we need to understand this as well. Every man has a story that God has written, and with your life you can use that story to engage others with the gospel of Jesus Christ.

Let me begin by sharing a few reasons why your story is important and why knowing how to communicate it is important as well.

- *It is unique.* There is no other story like yours. There are people out in the world waiting to hear a story like yours.

- *People can relate to it.* Everyone goes through ups and downs in life, and to hear a personal, honest story is refreshing.

- *No one can argue with it.* You can argue facts and theology, but no one can argue with what God has done in your life.

- *It is a window to Jesus.* They will see Jesus in the story. They will see the story of God all over it.

In his fantastic book *Just Walk Across the Room*, Bill Hybels challenged his congregation to write their story in a hundred words or less. A few years ago when preaching on Acts 26 where Paul shares his story, I made the same challenge to our congregation. Many people sent me their story and found the exercise helpful. Below are some guidelines to help get you started.

EXERCISE—PRESENTING YOUR STORY

1. Theme—Think about a central issue in your life that shows the contrast in your spiritual outlook before Christ and after meeting Christ.

    "I was striving . . . but now I'm grateful."

    "I was self-destructive . . . but now I'm healthy."

    "Guilty . . . but now liberated."

    "Fear-stricken . . . but now confident."

    "Despairing . . . but now hopeful."

2. Outline—Keep it clear and simple.

3. Conclusion—End with questions or a statement that requires a response.

4. Scripture—Think of one Bible verse that opened your eyes and share how it impacted you.

5. Length—Be brief and to the point.

6. Attitude—Share, don't preach!

7. Sensitivity—Focus on the other person and share aspects of your life that relate to his concerns and interests.

Assignment: Write your story in one hundred words or less.

PRINCIPLE #9: SHARE *the* STORY

When I was young, I believed there was only one way to share the gospel. As I matured in my faith and experienced different ministry organizations, as well as a variety of evangelism training, I realized there is more than one way to share the story. The most important principle to keep in mind is that it must feel comfortable to you.

Relax. Your job is not to convert the person; that is the job of the Holy Spirit. Too often we want to take over for the Holy Spirit and play the fourth part of the Trinity. We are continually thinking, *When should I lay it on him?* rather than allowing the Holy Spirit to take the relationship and conversation to the level he wants it to go.

Get rid of the God talk. If you have been a part of a church for a while you will have a tendency to use churchy language that those outside the church will find confusing or weird. As you learn a certain way of presenting the gospel, share it with a friend and ask him to do a friendly critique. Some words that can be scary or confusing are *washed in the blood, saved, redeemed, sanctified, purchased with a price, accept Jesus,* and many others.

Ask pilgrimage questions to get started. I will often ask questions to see if the person is interested in talking deeper about spiritual things. For example:

- Where are you in your spiritual journey or pilgrimage?
- How do you account for all the good things that have happened to you?
- What do you think is wrong with the world today?
- Why would something like that happen?
- Why do you think people do such terrible things?
- What do you think a Christian is?
- How can one possibly keep a family together these days?
- Sometime I would like to share some principles with you that will bring into focus what it means to know Christ personally; would this be a good time?

Pick a story. There are many ways to share the gospel, but here are two that I use on a regular basis:

"Do/Done"—I tell men that for years I was on the "Do" track, trying to earn God's love. But the problem was I never knew if I had done enough. I tell them religion is spelled D-O. I then write *Done* below *Do* and go on to tell them that Christianity is spelled D-O-N-E. Christ on the cross is enough; he did it all and there is nothing I can add to it. These two little words on a piece of paper can help men see the difference, and it also fits my testimony as well.

"The Bridge Diagram"—I learned this from the *Steps to Peace With God* booklet by the Billy Graham Association. I simply draw a bridge with God on one side and a man on the other side. I explain that God is someone who created us and loves us, but that sin entered the world and separated us from God. Man has made many attempts to get to the other side, but we always fall short. The only means to cross the chasm is Christ on the cross. The way one appropriates what Christ has done is to believe in him. The bridge God built is made of love, and all he asks us to do is walk across it by faith in him. Each aspect of this diagram has verses from the Scriptures that can be used to help explain it as well.

Whatever style or diagram you use, it is important to be biblical and logical. As I am explaining the gospel, I often ask if it makes sense or if they have any questions about what I am sharing. I want to make sure they fully grasp what I am saying.

I have covered a great deal of material in this chapter, and in some ways I have not done justice to the topic. If you are interested in further training in this area, there are lots of great books specifically on evangelism, including these I recommend:

Just Walk Across the Room by Bill Hybels
Becoming a Contagious Christian by Bill Hybels and Mark Mittelberg
The Coffeehouse Gospel by Matthew Paul Turner
Kingdom Come by Allen M. Wakabayashi
How to Give Away Your Faith by Paul Little
Out of the Salt Shaker and Into the World by Rebecca Pippert

NOTES

1. E. M. Bounds, *Power Through Prayer* (Grand Rapids: Baker Book House, 1971), 31.
2. Dan Spader, *Growing a Healthy Church: The Strategy of Jesus* (Elbrun, IL: Sonlife Ministries, 1998), 28.
3. George MacLeod, sermon, 1928.

05

A dad puts his child to bed at night, leaves the room, and goes downstairs. A bit later he hears a loud thud and runs back up to the child's room. Finding him on the floor he asks, "What happened?" The child answers, "I think I stayed too close to where I got in."

Isn't that true of so many Christian men today? They are staying too close to where they got in. They are missing the joy of walking with Christ in an intimate way. They aren't growing deeper with him, seeing their lives transformed, their relationships changed, or knowing the satisfaction of being involved in something much bigger than themselves.

In this chapter I will share some fundamental principles on spiritual growth and the ways God grows a man up into spiritual maturity.

Keep the End in Mind

The goal of one-on-one ministry is not to just get men into the pews on Sunday and keep them busy during the week with activities. The apostle Paul says in Colossians 1:28, "We proclaim him, admonishing and teaching everyone with all wisdom, so that we may present everyone perfect in Christ."

Did you notice that? Paul wanted to present *everyone* perfect in Christ. That word has gripped me over the past months. Paul's overriding goal was to see every man complete, mature in Christ. Becoming spiritually mature is not just for the elite, not just for those in the church, not just for those who feel like it. No, the word *everyone* means everyone! Not some, not a few, not almost all; it means every single man who is in our church or Bible study who names the name of Christ. Moving on to spiritual maturity is not an option, it is a mandate.

And when Paul said "perfect in Christ," he was not saying we have to be perfect, because we won't be this side of heaven. Rather, he was using a parenting analogy to get his point across. He was talking about people growing into spiritual adulthood, becoming like Christ, with their hearts and character transformed by him. Dallas Willard, in his wonderful book *The Renovation of the Heart*, describes it this way: "Spiritual formation is the Spirit driven process of forming the inner world of the human self in such a way that it becomes like the inner being of Christ himself."[1]

Paul was not interested in just helping people in times of crisis or helping them be better dads, husbands, or workers. He was not just looking for more volunteers for the local church. He desired every man to be more intimate with the Father, transformed from the inside out.

Unfortunately, too often in the church we settle for behavior modification rather than heart transformation. We settle for people just being good guys, who change their behavior a little bit so they fit into the cultural norms and standards of church life. I have news for you. God is not interested in good guys. He wants godly men. We have focused on externals rather than the heart and soul.

Paul talked about maturity a great deal in the Scriptures. For example, in 1 Corinthians 13:11, he said, "When I was a child, I talked like a child, I thought like a child, I reasoned like a child. When I became a man [or grew up], I put childish ways behind me." I don't know about you, but I know a lot of men who are in their forties, fifties, and sixties who are still acting, thinking, and talking like babies, and they are making baby messes all over the place!

John Stott, the great English preacher and writer, said the following at a missions conference at our church years ago: "For many years, twenty-five or more, the church-growth school has been dominant. I rejoice in the statistics, but we must say it is growth without depth." Chuck Colson was right when he said the church in America is three thousand miles wide and one inch deep. There are way too many babies in the church today.

A parent's job is to help his children grow up. We teach them how to eat, walk, read and write, run, ride a bike, earn money, study, and relate. It is a lifelong process of helping our children grow up so they can live on their own and not be dependent on their parents, but start a family of their own. It is no different in the church. Our job as shepherds is to help lots of big babies to grow up. To teach them how to feed themselves, walk on their own, find their place of service, and reproduce in others what you have done for them. Never lose sight of the goal.

Exercise (to be done individually or with others)

One problem in the church today is that of product. We don't know what we are trying to produce, so we are keeping men very busy with little life change and little resemblance to Jesus. Take time to think and study through what a "fully devoted follower of Jesus" looks like. What does Jesus say in the Gospels a disciple would be known for, do, and exhibit in his life? What would that look like today?

We Must Be Intentional

This past weekend in Chicago I had the privilege of watching my daughter Angie run her first marathon. Notice I said watch! I hate to run—always have and always will. Whenever I get a feeling that I should run, I lie down, take a nap, and get up when those feelings are gone. I can tell you right now that Angie did not get up that Sunday morning and decide at the last minute, "I think I'll run a marathon today with 37,000 other people." No, after running a couple of half marathons last year she followed a detailed training program set up by a professional runner. She gradually increased her miles, with long runs on the weekend, and then tapered as the race approached, all so she could be at her peak come race day. What a proud day for a parent to see his daughter run her heart out, work through the "wall," and finish what she started.

It is no different in the spiritual realm. You do not wake up one day spiritually mature. It goes without saying, we do not naturally drift toward maturity and Christlikeness. There has to be a deliberate plan; there has to be intentionality. Paul said he proclaimed Christ, "admonishing and teaching everyone" that they might be complete. In his book *Growing Disciples*, George Barna provides the staggering statistic that only three out of ten Christians have a plan for spiritual growth.[2] As adults we have a plan for just about everything else—losing weight, retirement, growing our children, growing our company, improving our golf game—but rarely do we have a plan to grow spiritually.

When it comes to working with men, you will want to have a plan for them to mature. There has to be a pathway for them to move from where they are to where God is taking them.

One thing I work with churches on is developing a pathway for growth that starts with new believers coming to Christ, learning the fundamentals of the faith, and then moving on to serve. We are building bridges for them to move from one thing to the next. For example, when we hold a GameDay breakfast, we encourage men to join an entry-level small group that has as its purpose an introduction to Jesus and small groups. This group will meet for eight weeks, with little to no homework. We make it an easy first step. Once completed, we ask them to make another commitment to a ten-week study with a few minutes of homework, and then after that a little bigger commitment. Hopefully during the course of these studies they'll take part in our leadership development track and become a small-group leader for others.

Everything we do has a purpose and is a part of the process of moving those babies in Christ to leaders in their homes, workplace, church, and community. But this does not just happen; it is a well-thought-out plan. What I am suggesting is that you think through the same thing for the men in your sphere. Start with where they are and move them along slowly. The important thing to keep in mind is that the Holy Spirit is at work, and you will want to listen and watch where God is working in the man's life so you can join in and work on issues relevant to him at that time.

Spiritual Formation Is a Process

Not only does there need to be a plan, but we need to view spiritual growth as a process. You cannot speed up the process. There is no such thing as microwaving Christians. God works differently in each person's life and he is not in a hurry, so we need to be patient.

I see four different stages of this process in Scripture. The first stage is when men are baby Christians and the cry of their heart is "feed me." In 1 Peter 2:2, Peter compares believers to newborn babies who long for the pure milk of the Word. In 1 Corinthians 3:1–3, Paul says there are some who are still on milk, not yet ready for solid food, still acting like babies. The primary need of this group is information about the new life in Christ and loving care to help them along. It is during this time when they are usually very hungry to grow and learn, and you do not want to waste this opportunity to get them involved in a basics of Christianity class or a discipleship relationship where they can be cared for and have their questions answered. It will be helpful for them to see the Christian life being lived out in others.

The second stage is the child Christian, and their cry is "teach me." Their primary need is the basic truths of the Bible and someone to explain them. They need unconditional love and protection. In 1 Corinthians 13:11, Paul says, "When I was a child, I talked like a child, I thought like a child, I reasoned like a child. When I became a man, I put childish ways behind me." Like children, men need to learn to feed themselves and walk on their own.

The third stage is the adolescent Christian, and their cry is "show me." Their primary need is to find victory over sin and develop a life of obedience to Christ. There will be an increased freedom and identity formation. The need to step out in faith will take encouragement from those working with them. In some ways you will serve as a coach to them with a hands-off approach. I once heard Tom Landry, the great coach of the Dallas Cowboys, say, "The job of a coach is making men do what they don't want to in order to become what they want to be." This type of relationship is seen in the bond between Paul and Timothy.

The fourth and final stage is the adult Christian, and their cry is "follow me." Their primary need is to use their gifts in ministry and begin training others. There is mutuality and reciprocity in the relationship; they are seen as peers. You become co-laborers in the cause of Christ (2 Corinthians 8:23; Philippians 2:25).

So what does all this mean for you as a leader of men? It means the men in your sphere of influence are likely at different points in their journey of faith, and there is no single correct approach for them all. You will be different things to different people.

Exercise

Take time to look at these four general categories of maturity and list where some of the men in your life are and what that means to your ministry to them.

	Men you know	What they need from you
Babies in Christ		
Children in Christ		
Adolescents in Christ		
Adult Christians		

Spiritual Formation Is Not Uniform

When I first got involved in campus ministry, it was implied that if I read the Bible and prayed, everything would be just fine and I would grow and become the person that God wanted me to be. There is truth to that, but what I have learned over the years in my own life and in working with others is that spiritual growth involves much more. I have learned that God is much bigger than we think, and he uses many ways to grow us up.

One exercise I like to use during training sessions is to have each man chart his life from birth to present, using symbols to represent key relationships, experiences, and circumstances that have been instrumental in his growth as a person. After twenty minutes or so, I will have the group shout out some of the key times in their life and I write them on the board. Inevitably they mention things like a Promise Keepers conference, losing their job, going through a divorce, an encouraging high school coach, the loss of a loved one, moving, changing jobs, getting married, a good friend or mentor . . . the list goes on and on. When it's full, I ask the men to look at it and tell me what they see. Almost every time there are three common denominators. First, it is not uniform— God uses a million and one ways to grow us. Second, usually there are very few "church activities" on the list, and third, it usually involves a great deal of pain. I include this exercise at the end of the chapter if you would like to work through it yourself.

One of the best authors on this subject and whose books I read as much as I can is Dallas Willard. He has been very instrumental in my own development as a follower of Christ. In one of his writings he talks about the Golden Triangle of Spiritual Growth.

The Golden Triangle

Dallas says there are basically three components of spiritual growth.

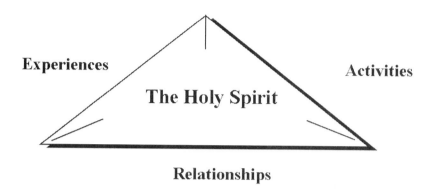

Experiences

Activities

The Holy Spirit

Relationships

1. Certain Relationships—Proverbs 27:17

Every man needs relationships that inspire, encourage, ask difficult questions, and provide counsel, support, and comfort. Christianity is not a solo sport; it is a team sport, and we need each other. I often tell the men of our church that isolation is not masculinity, it is stupidity! The optimal place for your growth is in a community of believers who will walk through life with you together. If you are not in a group, you are a moral accident ready to happen.

At a Promise Keepers conference years ago, Howard Hendricks of Dallas Theological Seminary said every man needs three types of relationships in his life: a Paul, a Barnabas, and a Timothy. A Paul is a mentor who inspires and provides advice. In Proverbs 19:20, the writer says to get all the advice you can and be wise the rest of your life. A Paul has been through battles in life and can provide perspective and counsel. A Paul can help us with our goals, roles, and souls. He wants to see you win in life. I have a number of Pauls in my life whom I talk with periodically. I talk to some about parenting issues, others about financial issues, others about my heart, and others about leadership issues. Each of these men desires to see me succeed, and I can ask them anything. They are not afraid to give it to me with the "bark on." In the same way that every professional athlete needs coaches, we need Pauls in our life.

A Barnabas is an encourager. The Barnabases in your life are peers who accept you for who you are. They are not impressed by what you do or what you have. They are men who are going in the same direction as you and want to help you achieve your mission in life. These are men you can meet with weekly in your small group, men who are your friends, men who will support and encourage you when you are hurting.

The third group of people we need in our lives are Timothys. These are the men you are building your life into. You may be working with high school or college students, a group of men at the local prison, or a men's small group. These are relationships where you become the Paul to them. Through these relationships you will learn to serve and be dependent on the Holy Spirit, and you will have to prepare and give of yourself for the good of others.

A few years ago a couple of friends convinced me to take up biking. Not the Harley-Davidson type of biking, but the bicycling type. They picked me up early one Saturday, and yes, I even wore those stretchy pants. What a sight that was! We went out into the country and the five of us took off for a twenty-five-mile ride. By mile five I was ready for a spa and a nap, and received neither. Around mile fifteen I heard a loud sound that was similar to what you hear when a tornado is approaching, but the sky was clear. The guys told me to pull over and watch what was coming. No sooner had I pulled off to the side and looked back when I saw about seventy-five cyclists coming around the corner. They were bunched together and practically flying. After they passed I asked one of the big-time riders what it was like to ride in a pack like that. He said there was nothing else like it. When you are in the middle you are literally being pulled along by the other bikers, and they take turns going up front and leading the pack because that is the hardest position.

As I think about that experience, I think that is exactly what the relationships in our life is like. It is a picture of the church. We are all heading in the same direction, but there are times when we need to be out front and times when we need to be in the middle of the pack, being pulled along by others. God uses all our relationships to mold us, shape us, challenge us, and form us into his image.

2. Certain Experiences—1 Peter 4:12

In the same way that God uses a variety of relationships in our life, he will use a variety of experiences as well. One of those experiences is suffering. None of us would sign up for suffering, nor would we probably buy a book on the subject, but there is no doubt that it is one of God's great instruments for shaping us and deepening us. It is through suffering and pain that God touches our soul. Paul, in Philippians 1:29, says that it has been granted to us not only to believe but also to suffer, and then in 1 Peter 4:12, Peter says not to be surprised when you suffer.

Suffering, setbacks, and pain are a part of life, and God is going to use them in each of our lives. The only wasted pain is the pain that we do not learn and grow through. The great pastor and writer A. W. Tozer said, "It is doubtful that God can use any man greatly, until he has been hurt deeply."[3]

A few years ago I was invited by the Marines to address the leaders of the Pacific Fleet and speak to the Marines stationed at the air station training base at Miramar. One group was new recruits, fresh off the bus. I had just finished speaking at their chapel when a young rookie Marine came up to talk and quickly started to cry. This was not expected and a little disconcerting. He looked me in the eyes and said he wanted to quit and go home. Not thinking it was an option, I called over the sergeant who was hosting me for the week and asked if he would join the conversation. He told the young man that the goal of the drill instructor was to break him, take away his identity, and give him a new one. He described it like refining metal. You are in a crucible and they are going to heat you up, and when the impurities come to the top they will skim them off with a knife. Then they will heat it up again and skim it off again. They will do this until that drill instructor can look down into that crucible and see his reflection in you. He told the young man that the DI was not interested in his happiness or comfort but in his becoming a Marine.

As I listened to the sergeant, I realized that is exactly what God is doing in our lives. We are in the crucible and he is going to heat it up and skim off the impurities and then heat it up again until Jesus can look down and see his reflection in our lives. He is refining us like gold, transforming us into his image. Like the DI, Jesus wants to see his reflection in us. Like the DI, Jesus is not interested in our happiness but our godliness. The application when working with men is to use the pain they are going through to lead them into a deeper walk with Jesus. Take time to talk about it, pray about it, and walk with them through it.

I mentioned earlier that men like action. Many men learn best through experience rather than through books. It is no wonder God will use our service to others as a catalyst to change us. I have found that it is one thing to have men attend a Bible study—it is completely another to get one to lead a Sunday school class, work on a Habitat for Humanity project, feed the needy at the rescue mission, or play basketball in a prison. When you get men out of their comfort zone, they are placed in a position where they have to trust God, get dirty, and humble themselves.

One thing I regularly do is take men overseas on missions trips. I will tell you right now that they get much more out of it than what they do for others. I can still remember a small group of men who went to the Philippines with me to do a construction project that was not quite ready to be worked on when we arrived. At first all these type-A men were frustrated, a little angry, and just wanted to go home. So I prayed with them and encouraged them to open their eyes and wait on God to see how he would use them in the next week. And boy, did he use them in ways they never imagined. That Sunday one of the men walked into a small church to share his testimony, and when the pastor saw him come in, the pastor informed him he would be preaching that morning—not just sharing his testimony! To see Dave on his knees in the back praying for a message was a real joy to me. I could have never planned this type of experience, but God could.

3. Certain Activities—1 Timothy 4:7

Paul says in 1 Timothy 4:7 to train yourself for godliness, and he goes on to say that physical training has some value, but spiritual training has value in all things. The word *train* comes from the word *gumanzo*, from which we get gymnasium. It brings with it the idea of sustained effort toward a goal. The goal is godliness and ordering our life around Christ and his values and way of life. What Paul is saying is that in the same way it takes years of training to become a world-class athlete, it takes years of training to become a spiritual champion. Paul draws upon an event they would all be aware of—the Isthmian games in Corinth. People would go through ten months of rigorous training on their own, and, if selected, they would train for a month with a personal trainer in Corinth. Any success was dependent on the intensity of the training. The application for us is that if we are going to be like Jesus on the field, then we must be like him off the field. We are going to partake in the daily regimens that Jesus did, and these are the spiritual disciplines.

John Ortberg, in his book *The Life You've Always Wanted*, defines a spiritual discipline as "any activity that can help me gain power to live life as Jesus taught and modeled it."[4] In our working with men, we will put a priority on helping men to incorporate the various disciplines into their life. Disciplines such as silence, study, worship, prayer, journaling, fasting, and service enable men to hear God's voice, sense his presence, experience his power, and become like him.

I have found that you cannot have a man just read a book about prayer, Bible study, silence, or solitude and expect him to practice that discipline on a regular basis. A better way is to take time either one-on-one or in a small group and go through a devotional together for several weeks to actually practice what you are discussing. After that you may want to start your group time by asking the men what the Lord has been teaching them through their Scripture reading and prayer time. You might consider fasting together the day of your study and then discussing how it went, or taking a Saturday and having a silent retreat together. In all of these types of experiential activities, men move from information to practice to transformation. When men get to the point where they have built a rhythm of disciplines, they will discover the incredible joy of walking with the Lord, hearing from the Lord, and being transformed by him.

The Work of the Holy Spirit

Take another look at the Golden Triangle diagram and you will notice the Holy Spirit in the middle. Spiritual growth is not a formula, it is not impossible, and it is not a mere human activity. Spiritual growth is the work of the Holy Spirit in the life of the believer. The Scriptures tell us that the moment we commit our lives to Jesus, the Holy Spirit comes into our lives and seals us as children of God. From that time forward the Spirit is working out his purposes in our life. He is helping us in times of temptation, giving us strength when we are weak, providing wisdom when making decisions, convicting us when we sin, and slowly but surely transforming us into the image of Jesus. Someone once said that spiritual growth is more similar to sailing than to driving a car. When driving, you are in control and you go where you want to go. With sailing, you turn the sails into the wind, and the wind takes you where it wants to go. Growing into spiritual maturity is more of a journey than a destination. It is daily surrendering your life to him, getting off the throne of your life, and allowing the Holy Spirit to work in and through you.

An important component of allowing the Spirit to work is that of confession of sin—taking the time to ask the Holy Spirit to shine the light of his holiness into your life and show you where you are missing the mark, and then taking the time to confess it to God and ask his forgiveness and strength to turn from it.

Exercise

Who is a Paul in your life?

Who is a Barnabas in your life?

Who is a Timothy in your life?

How can you help another man (or men) develop these types of relationships?

What are some ways you can get men out of their comfort zone to serve?

Where do you need to grow in the area of spiritual disciplines?

How did you learn the various disciplines and how do you plan to help others grow in this area?

THE OPTIMAL PLACE FOR SPIRITUAL GROWTH IS IN A SMALL GROUP

The final point I want to make in this chapter is that the optimal place for a man to grow is in a small group. I know I touched on this earlier when talking about the different types of relationships we need in our life, but I want to mention it again. Everything we do as a ministry to men at Elmbrook is geared toward encouraging men to become involved in small groups, because we feel so strongly about it. We're a big church and have all types of groups, whether it is a support group, a task group, a Bible study group, an entry-level group, a mission group, a leadership development group, a No Regrets study group (our discipleship group), or an IronMan group. Whatever the type, whenever they meet, the common thread is men sharpening one another. It is a place where the men can be comforted when they walk through the valley of the shadow of death, a place to be encouraged when they take a step of faith or say no to sin, a place where their faith can be fanned into flames, and a place where their gifts can be discovered and used. It is a place where they can do life together, where they can love, forgive, accept, and carry one another's burdens. There is absolutely nothing like a men's small group running on all cylinders, where men catch a passion for God and what God wants to do in their lives. When this starts to happen, get out of the way.

NOTES

1. Dallas Willard, *The Renovation of the Heart* (Colorado Springs: NavPress, 2002), 22.

2. George Barna, *Growing Disciples* (Colorado Springs: Waterbrook Press, 2001), 38.

3. A. W. Tozer, *The Root of the Righteous* (Camp Hill, PA: Christian Publications, 1955), 137.

4. John Ortberg, *The Life You've Always Wanted* (Grand Rapids: Zondervan, 2002), 48.

How to Disciple a Man

06

It all started when I first came to the Lord as a senior in high school. John, the college student who led me to the Lord, spent six months meeting with me on a weekly basis, if not more, to instruct me and build into me the basics of being a disciple of Jesus. Through Bible study, long walks together, serving together, and learning to share my faith, he helped me see that to be a follower of Jesus was an adventure, a lifetime commitment, and I had the responsibility to do for others what he did for me.

Early on we walked through Robert Coleman's wonderful book *The Master Plan of Evangelism*, and through that I discovered that Jesus' entire ministry was predicated on building into twelve men who the multitudes would follow. One quote that really made an impact on me and has impacted my entire ministry is, "One must decide where he wants his ministry to count—in the momentary applause of popular recognition or the reproduction of his life in a few chosen men who will carry on his work after he is gone. Really it is a question of which generation we are living for."[1]

When Stuart Briscoe asked me to head Elmbrook's men's ministry in 1992, I was completely unsure what to do and where to start. Stuart's advice? "Do the same thing you've been doing with the college-age students; just try to act a little more mature!" We had discipled the college kids in small groups, so I started doing the same with men.

After surveying the lay of the land, so to speak, I discovered three things: a lack of godliness among men, a lack of men involved in the church, and a lack of male leadership. There was only one thing to do: start a movement of discipleship among the men. So I asked twelve men to join me on Wednesday mornings and another group of men to join a good friend of mine on Tuesday mornings. For the next nine months we poured our lives into those twenty-four men. We met with them weekly, prayed with them, studied the Word with them, were mutually accountable to one another, went to ball games together, cried together, and walked through some of the most difficult times together. This was no easy feat as we asked the men to commit to two hours in class and two hours of homework.

Many people around the country told me I was crazy. They told me men don't like to read, men won't get up early, men won't memorize Scripture, men won't be accountable to one another, and the list went on and on! Well, thirty-six weeks later we finished the first year of Basic Training and were twenty-four for twenty-four. They all loved it so much they wanted to take another group of men through the process. The next year we had nine groups, the following year twelve, then fifteen, and the process continued for the next ten years; close to eight hundred men have been discipled. The church has never been the same.

Alan Hirsch, in his book *The Forgotten Ways,* says it this way: "The quality of a church's leadership is directly proportional to the quality of its discipleship. If we fail in the area of making disciples, we should not be surprised if we fail in the area of leadership development. I think many of the problems the church faces in trying to cultivate missional leadership for the challenges of the twenty-first century would be resolved if we were to focus the solution to the problem on something prior to leadership development per se, namely, that of discipleship first. Discipleship is primary; leadership is always secondary. . . . The reach of any movement is directly proportional to the breadth of its leadership base. And leadership in turn is directly related to the quality of discipleship."[2]

What we soon discovered was the discipleship we were doing with the men resulted in their finding their place of service all over the church and in turn their place of leadership in the home, church, workplace, and world. The movement of discipleship we started in the early nineties has served to be the model and impetus for all we have done in our ministry. It was slow, it was intentional, and it was deep. We were never concerned with numbers but with building men who loved Jesus and others. With such pressure today to preach like the greats around the country or to have a mega-church, it is hard to remember the simple mandate that Jesus gave us two thousand years ago to make disciples.

Early in my ministry I resolved not to be concerned with the multitudes, with the bigger and better, but rather taking the time to build into a small group of high school students, college students, and now men who would do the same in the lives of others. It is an incredible joy to look back over these years and see so many students and men who have gone on to be fully devoted followers of Jesus and are seeking to do the same in the lives of others. For me, this is one of the most exciting chapters in the book as I get to lay out some basic principles that have been foundational for my life and ministry over the past thirty-five years.

Discipleship = Spiritual Depth

So few people in our churches have been discipled that we now have a problem with our "product"—with the way people are living. Without a clear and compelling vision of discipleship, there is no depth in the lives of our people, and our churches have little impact in the world. I believe that Howard Hendricks said it best when he said, "The church will not survive without discipleship."[3]

Jesus gave a clear command two thousand years ago: "Go and make disciples" (Matthew 28:19). So often we hear the emphasis on this passage being to go to the far reaches of the world, but this is not the main verb of the passage. The main verb is to "make disciples." The three ways you do that is to go, baptize, and teach, and this speaks of process.

The word *disciple* was not a new word for the disciples of Jesus. It was commonly used by great teachers and philosophers of the time. To be a disciple was to first be a follower. This of course meant the students would closely follow after the teacher. Jesus did not call them to a set of teachings but to himself. To follow was to leave the former way of life and imitate the one you are following. Second, it meant to be a learner. To be a learner was to sit at the feet of the teacher and learn from him. A key characteristic of any disciple is his teachability. We are to perpetuate the learning process, and this means we will never stop learning.

Finally, to be a disciple meant to be a reproducer. This meant to reproduce the life of the teacher in others. We are to be equippers and trainers of others so they can continue the process. Teaching them to lead someone to Christ is not enough; they must do it themselves. Jesus picks up on this idea and says our responsibility is to go into the world and help men be followers, learners, and reproducers of Jesus. It is a matter of product. When working with men we need to keep the end game in mind—what are we trying to produce? Are we happy with men who at one time in their life made a commitment to Jesus and now are living with little or no evidence of that profession? Or do we want to see men who are following hard after Jesus, who are perpetuating the learning process and are becoming more and more like Jesus every day? I don't know about you, but I want to see men whose minds are being renewed, lives transformed, and the world impacted for Jesus. And it all starts with discipleship.

Paul had the very same vision. In 2 Timothy 2:2, when speaking to his young protégé, Timothy, he says, "And the things you have heard me say in the presence of many witnesses entrust to reliable men who will also be qualified to teach others." Paul is speaking of four generations of men here. It starts with Paul, who has invited Timothy to join him in Acts 16, and for the next ten years they have been ministering together, going city to city to plant churches. During that time Paul has instructed Timothy in the basics of Christianity. He has helped Timothy to discover his gifts and use them for the extension and expansion of the kingdom of God. He now tells Timothy that the things he has seen and heard in Paul's life should be passed on to others, who in turn will pass them on to others. This is the ministry of multiplication that was seen and taught by Jesus and was now modeled and taught by Paul. Nowhere do we see instructions of how the church should be about adding just one member at a time. Rather, we see the principle of multiplication from beginning to end. God is a God of multiplication. On a wall in the

Museum of Natural Science in Chicago there is a checkerboard with sixty-four squares. In the lower left-hand corner is a grain of wheat. The display includes this question: "If you doubled the amount of wheat as you move from square to square, how much would you have when you reached the sixty-fourth square? A carload? A trainload? You would have enough wheat to cover the country of India six feet deep."

This is the power of multiplication; this is what can happen when we catch a vision for discipleship with men.

Principles of Discipleship

There is absolutely no getting around it—if we are going to leave a legacy, it will be when we make disciples, who make disciples, who make disciples. It is possible to lead a man to Christ in twenty minutes, but it can take at least half a year to help him grow in Christian maturity.

The first question we have to ask is, what does it mean to disciple men? Greg Ogden in his book *Discipleship Essentials* defines discipleship as "an intentional relationship in which we walk alongside other disciples in order to encourage, equip, and challenge one another in love to grow toward maturity in Christ. This includes equipping the disciple to teach others as well."[4] Some key concepts to discipleship are worth emphasizing and serve as a good lead-in for how to get started in this life-changing process.

- *Intentionality.* There needs to be a purposeful plan to invest your life in the lives of others. It is not going to just happen.

- *Relationship.* It is not a program but a relationship you are inviting the men into.

- *Walk alongside of them.* It is not a race or an unloading of everything you know, but there is a sense of mutuality, of walking together through life.

- *Maturity in Christ.* This is the end game. Keep in mind the goal is to see men grow up in Christ. Discipleship is about transformation, not just imparting information.

> ■ *Equipping them to do for others what you have done for them.* This again speaks to the concept of multiplication. You have not fully discipled another man until he is doing for others what you did for him.

Identify a Few

One question I often hear is, "Who should I disciple?" I believe that we are to take our cue from Jesus, who spent an entire night in prayer before asking the original disciples to join him. Now, you may not spend an entire night praying, but I would definitely make it a regular part of your prayer time. Ask God to direct you to the right men and give you some divine appointments and connections. You may want to start making a list of men you will be praying for. The men you disciple are going to come from several areas. Your first and probably best source are men with whom you have developed a relationship.

I encourage our men to view our activities as a fishing pond where they can look for men to disciple. If a man is attending an event, there may already be an interest in spiritual things, and we can help him take the next step. For example, if you have a mens' retreat, don't sit with all your buddies at mealtime; rather, look for men who are by themselves and spend time getting to know them. You will also want to strike when the iron is hot. At the end of the retreat, make sure to provide an opportunity for men to join a discipleship group.

For every activity, be sure to build a bridge to discipleship groups. The same can be said of a worship service. Sunday is an excellent chance to get to know new men and ask them to join you. A second way to find men to disciple is through the process your church may already have in place for discipleship. For example, we have a team of men who disciple men after they become believers. This team is also available to have men referred to them for the follow-up process. If you are unsure who needs to be discipled, ask your pastor or other leaders for the names of men who are new to the faith and need help getting started. Finally, as you lead men to Christ, take the responsibility to disciple them as well.

When looking for men to pour my life into, I always look for three qualities. I am not sure who came up with this, but it has been around for years and it still works for me. I look for men who are FAT.

Faithful—If you set up a meeting, they will be there. If you ask them to do something, they do it.

Available—They are available to meet on a weekly basis. Many men today are so busy they don't make meeting a priority, and they always have an excuse.

Teachable—They want to learn and grow. These men come prepared, have lots of questions, and have a teachable spirit, not a know-it-all attitude.

Having prayed for and identified the men for a group, I will then extend a personal invitation for them to join a small group with me. I have found a good size for a group is five to eight so each man has a chance to participate. I have also found that long-term discipleship is best when done in small groups rather than exclusive one-on-one relationships. I am not against one-on-one discipleship, but I find with groups there can be less of a dependency on the leader and more opportunity for men to learn from each other. It also takes away the danger of mirroring, which can occur in a one-on-one relationship.

Invitation to a Relationship, Not a Program

When you make the invitation for a man to join your discipleship group, you are inviting him into a relationship, not to a program. They do not want to feel they are on a production line, but rather in a long-term relationship based on honesty, authenticity, and love. In Mark 3:14, Jesus invited the disciples to be *with* him. You are inviting men to be *with* you.

Instruct in the Basics

When one looks at Jesus, he was continually teaching the disciples the values and ways of the kingdom of God. Now, his teaching style was a bit different from what we think of when we think of discipleship.

We normally think of having a three-ring binder filled with notes, or a manual where we answer questions, or a book we read. On the other hand, Jesus taught in many ways and in many places. He used parables for some, a stormy sea for others, miracles for others, and even large-group teaching time. There wasn't just one way he used to impart the basics of followership to the disciples; he used a multitude of ways to grow them in their faith. The same will be true of us. There is no one way, no magic bullet to disciple your men. When it comes to building the basics into your men, there are a few areas you'll want to develop.

1. *Help them cultivate an eternal perspective.* This involves helping men develop a Christian worldview so they are viewing all of life through the lens of Scripture. In Romans 12:1–2, Paul challenges us to be "transformed by the renewing of [our] mind." As we go through the discipleship process we will want to help them develop the thought process rather than just skills. Viewing life through Scripture will impact their job, their family, how they vote, how they spend their finances, and how they serve in the world.

2. *Help them cultivate godly character.* This of course means helping them begin to live in obedience to Jesus in every area of their lives. They will learn to deny themselves and take up the cross and follow Christ daily. Through discussion, accountability, study, and prayer, you will be able to discuss how Christianity intersects with their lives in a very practical way.

3. *Help them love as Jesus loved.* Jesus loved the poor and the wealthy, the sick and the healthy, the educated and the uneducated. A major part of the discipleship process is to help men grow in their love for others. It is in relationship where the rubber meets the road with Christianity. Will they be able to forgive a family member who has wronged them? Will they be able to accept a child's friend who is different?

4. *Help them cultivate the spiritual disciplines to walk with Jesus.* A major part of the process will help them build into their daily and weekly lives the disciplines of Bible study, prayer, journaling, silence, and solitude. The goal is to have men who can walk with Jesus on their own and not need to be spoon-fed.

5. *Help them discover their place of service.* Helping men discover and develop their spiritual gifts is one aspect of the process that is often ignored and yet is so important if we are going to mobilize this great army of men. We will spend the next chapter expanding on this because it is so important.

6. *Help them become a servant leader.* Jesus was a servant leader, and the discipleship process is empowering our men to be servant leaders in their families, workplace, church, community, and world. I know from experience that this has been a revolutionary thought for men to apply to the marketplace.

With these principles in mind, allow me to mention some of the materials/tools we have used with our men.

- *Operation Timothy* by Christian Businessmen's Connection— Three male-friendly booklets cover the basics very well. They help men grow in intimacy with Christ and into mature followers of Christ. These studies are taken from the Navigators' Design for Discipleship series. You can find more information at www.operationtimothy.com, or you can pick them up at most Christian bookstores.

- *Discipleship Essentials* by Greg Ogden—This twenty-four-week manual involves Scripture memory, Bible study, and a short reading. It may be a little long for a man who has never been involved in something like this before, but the material is well worth it. It can be used in a one-on-one setting, in a triad, or in a small group.

- *Growing in Christ* by NavPress—This booklet is only thirteen weeks long and is a good tool for getting started. It begins with assurance of salvation and then moves into how to grow as believer.

- *IronMan* by No Regrets Men's Ministry—A nine-week guide that covers the basics of what it means to follow Christ.

One reason I like using a booklet such as the ones listed is that the study is more intentional. They provide a pathway for the men to move through the topics they need.

From Instruction to Involvement

If discipleship were dependent on just passing on information, this country would have the greatest disciples in the world. We are great at going to seminars, taking notes, accumulating binders, and filling our heads with information. But as we have discussed, this is not what discipleship is about. It is about the transformation of a life. To that end, if our discipleship is going to be effective, it must be experiential in nature and preparing men to do for others what you did for them. The discipleship must take place in the context of life and be worked out in the daily activities and experiences of their life.

Again, the model that Jesus gives us in the Gospels is the place to start. He provides the framework for how we can move the men from instruction to involvement. As I look at his method, there seems to be four stages in the discipleship process.

The first stage is the instruction stage. It is in this stage that he taught them about prayer, love, character, faith, heaven, and many other key kingdom issues. Jesus used a wide variety of teaching styles to convey the lessons he had for his men.

The second stage is the illustration stage: Jesus was a living example of the lessons he was teaching them. For example, in Luke 11 the disciples were walking along the road when they came across Jesus in prayer. They had a chance to listen and watch as he prayed. Throughout his life they saw him living in intimate relationship with the Father, and so when he spoke about it, they knew exactly what that looked like in real life. When he spoke to them about love and compassion, they knew what that looked like because they saw a man who loved everyone he came in contact with.

The third stage is the involvement stage. He did not stop at instructing and illustrating, but rather sent them out to do it as well. In the same way you cannot learn to swim by a correspondence course, you cannot become a fully devoted follower of Jesus by just reading a book. You need to jump in and do it. That is why in Luke 10 Jesus sends the disciples out two by two to minister. They come back and he debriefs them, and they go out again. Jesus used this experiential style of training all through his ministry. I would suggest there were four phases Jesus walked them through:

I do—you watch
I do—you help
You do—I help (This was normally in a controlled situation.)
You do—I watch (This was normally in their everyday life.)

Allow me to share an example of what that could look like in a discipleship group. Let's say you are helping the men write their testimony so they can share it with others. You might begin by giving them some simple how-tos of writing and giving a testimony. Then you would share your testimony with them to give them an example of what it looks like. Give them time to write theirs out in class, then give them a chance to run it by you and the group to make sure it flows and does not have too much religious jargon, etc. Then give each guy a chance to share it in a safe environment, which would be the group. Provide feedback if they need to refine it. You might also have them share their testimony at a men's breakfast. Again, this is a pretty safe environment since it is predominately Christian men. Finally, you might look for some opportunities for them to share it in public. You will notice there is a nice progression here of instructing them, giving them an example, allowing them to present it in a safe environment, and then going out on their own. You could take every aspect of discipleship and apply this principle to it. If we don't, it simply becomes head knowledge.

Related to this, one of the underlying things you will want to do with your men is cultivate their faith whenever and wherever possible. By putting them in situations where they need to step out in obedience, say no to sin, or incorporate something into their lives, you are giving them a chance to deepen their faith in God and their dependence on God. Again, this moves discipleship from being purely head knowledge to transformational ministry.

Let me close this chapter by telling you about one of my ministry heroes at Elmbrook. For the past fifteen years Mike has been meeting with a rotating group of four to five men at the local Perkins restaurant. What these men have in common is they have all just come into a relationship with the Lord and are in desperate need of someone to disciple them. They usually stay with Mike for six months to a year as he works through the *Operation Timothy* booklets with them. Besides their weekly study, he spends time with them outside the group talking, counseling, and living life together. For many men in our area, Mike is the one who put legs to their faith and equipped them to walk with Jesus on their own. When Mike is asked about his personal ministry, he says simply, "I'm doing what Jesus commanded us all to do. To make disciples, who make disciples, who make disciples."

Exercise—Praying for Men to Disciple

Who are the men you want to start praying for right now that God may want you to invite into a discipleship group?

1.

2.

3.

4.

5.

Discussion Questions

1. Share your experience in either being discipled or discipling another man.
2. Discuss how spiritual multiplication is different from addition.
3. Why is it so hard for the people in the church to understand the vision and method of discipleship?
4. What would a focus on discipleship look like in your ministry?

NOTES

1. Robert Coleman, *The Master Plan of Evangelism* (Old Tappan, NJ: Revell, 1963), 37.

2. Alan Hirsch, *The Forgotten Ways* (Grand Rapids: Brazos Press, 2006), 119.

3. Howard Hendricks, lecture at Bethel Seminary.

4. Greg Ogden, *Discipleship Essentials* (Downers Grove: InterVarsity Press, 1998), 17.

07

Sports were my god when I was growing up. I was always in someone's backyard playing football, on someone's driveway shooting hoops, or at the local park playing baseball. We would play in the heat, in the rain, and in the snow, wherever and whenever we could. Not only did I play a ton of sports, I have been to a ton of games. My father would take me to see the Milwaukee Braves in my younger years, and then later the Brewers. I had the opportunity to see World Series games and All Star games. I spent countless nights at the Milwaukee Arena watching Al McGuire coach Marquette and Don Nelson coach the Milwaukee Bucks. And throughout the years, I went to hundreds of Badgers games in Madison and a number of Green Bay Packers games.

It was great watching a World Series game against the Cardinals and the Packers against the Vike-queens, but let me tell you, I would much rather be in the action than just watching it! Being a spectator never compares with the thrills and chills of being in the game. I would much rather get a little banged up in a pickup basketball game than sipping a Coke in the stands.

Church should be the same way. Men might be used to the stands, but that doesn't mean they should stay there or that they like it. All they usually need is some encouragement and perhaps training to use their gifts, talents, abilities, and passions to get into the game and expand the kingdom of God.

We are Built for Service

In college I had the incredible opportunity to be an assistant football coach at my old high school. We had a saying: Everyone is a starter and has a role to play. We continually reminded the young men of this because you never knew how the game would progress or when someone would be injured. We told the players there was no such thing as second string; they were all starters and would need to contribute at some time if we were going to be successful.

To effectively mobilize men for kingdom service, we need to believe that every man is a starter in the church. The most powerful verse regarding this is Ephesians 2:10, where Paul says, "We are God's workmanship, created in Christ Jesus to do good works, which God prepared in advance for us to do." The word *workmanship* is literally the word *masterpiece*. In God's eyes, we are a Picasso or a Rembrandt. And God has designed and created us for a specific job and a unique role in his redemptive plans for the world.

I believe one big reason men are not serving in the church today is because we have ignored Ephesians 2:10. We do not consider men masterpieces. Instead, we simply try to fill open spots with warm bodies, and it has done nothing but frustrate everyone. Men hear the pleas from the pulpit for helpers over and over again. Finally, at a point of weakness and incredible shame, they sign up to help in the children's nursery. They have no interest, no passion, no talent or gifting in the area, but they do it to appease the guilt and shame they are feeling. They put in their three months and then run for the hills, promising themselves they will never do that again!

Friends, there is a better way, and it starts with believing in the core of our being that our chief job is to equip others. We need to change how we measure success in the church from "what I do" to "who I equip." It does not take a brain surgeon to understand that as one man, you will be very limited in what you can do. But if you equip and mobilize a hundred men in your lifetime, the impact will be much greater and far-reaching. So how are you viewing men these days? As starters wanting to get into the game, or as bench sitters watching you do everything? If you are interested in getting men out of the pews and into the game, allow me to share some principles I have found extremely helpful over the years.

Prayer. No matter the situation, everything about ministry to men should start with prayer. In Matthew 9:37–38, Jesus tells the disciples that the harvest is plentiful. That's true in our day as well. But what is the first thing he tells them to do? Hire a headhunter? No! The first step is to pray to the Lord of the harvest to send workers *for* the harvest. Whenever I see someone in church who isn't involved but should be, I put his name on a list and begin to pray for him. I regularly pray through this list, asking God to thrust these people into the harvest—maybe in the men's ministry or some other area of service. When our leadership team meets, we start with prayer and ask the Lord of the harvest to send men into the harvest fields. Start praying for men to get out of the pews and into the game.

Vision. I have talked about vision before, but I mention it again because of its importance in mobilizing men. There are three ways to effectively share a vision that has eternal consequences.

First, as a leader, you need to embody the vision. For example, when former president Jimmy Carter does an interview for Habitat for Humanity, he is seldom in a suit and tie. He is almost always in his jeans with a tool belt around his waist. President Carter embodies the vision of Habitat by spending a great deal of time each year pounding nails. To embody the vision of service for your men means you will not just talk about serving the poor; you *will* serve the poor. You will not just talk about overseas missions; you will be *involved* in overseas missions.

Second, you will want to share the vision publicly. Whether from the pulpit on a Sunday morning, at a men's breakfast on a Saturday morning, or in a monthly newsletter, etc., men should hear your vision regularly so they know exactly where the ministry is going.

A third way is to share the vision one-on-one with a man. There is nothing like sitting across from a man at breakfast and sharing the vision of the church and/or ministry and letting him know what role he can play in the fulfillment of that vision. Some of my best conversations with men have come during these sorts of meetings. No matter what the setting, we need to let men know what "hill" we are climbing and invite them to join us.

Relationship. Once again, *relationship* needs to be emphasized. It is much easier to ask a man to join you in ministry or get involved if there is an existing relationship rather than just a call out of the blue. We have found that men will generally not respond to an ad in the bulletin or a pulpit announcement, but they will typically respond to a relationship. These relationships can be developed in many ways. It could be as simple as talking to a man before or after service and asking him about his life, interests, and passions. I also call men I don't know well and ask if we can meet to get to know one another. At first they think I want something from them, but I let them know all I want is for them to share their story with me and vice versa. I believe it was John Maxwell who said years ago, "You never ask for the hand until you get to know the heart."

S.H.A.P.E. Every coach knows a team won't work properly unless each player is in the right place doing the right thing. It is no different in the church. Each man in your church has a sweet spot, a place where he will be most effective. Part of a leader's responsibility is to help guys find their spot. I really like the paradigm Saddleback Church in California uses under the leadership of Erik Rees. The following information is from Erik's book *S.H.A.P.E.: Finding and Fulfilling Your Unique Purpose for Life.*

S—Spiritual Gifts. The Holy Spirit gives every believer some spiritual gift for the "common good" (1 Corinthians 12:7), including the gifts of administration, discernment, teaching, mercy, giving, evangelism, encouragement, helps, leadership, healing, and faith. Step one in discovering what role God has for a man is identifying his spiritual gifts.

H—Heart Passion. Next, help a man discover the passion of his heart. What does he get excited about? Perhaps there's a social issue he wants to conquer, such as abortion, divorce, or poverty, or perhaps he finds himself wanting to help meet a need in people, whether physical, relational, spiritual, vocational, or another type. I'll tell you this: The ultimate contribution God wants from a man will align with the passions God has given that man.

A—Abilities. Natural abilities are a part of every man's heavenly shape. Some men are good with numbers, sports, singing, mechanics, strategizing, performing, writing, leading, computing, welcoming, designing, landscaping, building, cooking, coaching, or planning. We need to remind men that every ability they have can be used for God's glory. A good friend of mine was a fantastic athlete in high school and college. During seminary, he started coaching the local high school basketball team. Twenty years later, coaching mainly on a volunteer basis, he has had an incredible ministry to hundreds and hundreds of student athletes. The abilities your men have are a strong indication of what God wants to do with their life.

P—Personality. God loves variety. Everywhere you look in creation you see variety, from spiders to zebras, from giant Sequoias to roses. It is the same with human beings. Like stained glass, our personalities reflect God's light in so many colors and patterns. God has instilled a unique personality in each of us for his glory. And being true to who God made us is of utmost importance. Help your men understand they do not have to become someone they are not in order to serve God. There is no right or wrong personality type.

E—Experiences. God uses our life experiences for the role he has us play. He uses painful and joyful times to flesh out a finished product. He sees our life from start to finish and will put us through a storm at age thirty in order that we might survive a hurricane at age sixty. God never wastes a hurt, and most likely it will be the basis of a great ministry.

Ask. Bill Hybels said at a Leadership Summit years ago, "Nothing in the kingdom of God ever gets done without an ask." Too often we expect men just to sign up and start serving. This is not going to happen. I usually meet men at their work or in my office, or we get together for a meal. In doing this we can connect face-to-face. I tell them that I have been praying about their involvement in the church and feel it's time to talk about it. I share the vision for an area of ministry and where we are going—the big picture. We like men to connect to a vision, not a program. Once they grasp the big picture, I share more specifically about the area where I see them becoming involved. It could be heading up small-group ministry, leading a small group, planning a retreat, or teaching a Sunday school class. I let them know my perspective of why I think they are the right person to serve in this area and how they would fit on the team. At this one-on-one meeting we also talk about the specifics of the position.

After walking through the position description, we discuss any questions he may have. We end our conversation by praying; I ask him to pray about the opportunity. If he's married, I ask him to talk with his wife before making a commitment. He is then given a specific time frame of when I need his response—usually a week to two.

Just do it. With all of this in mind, we have found the best thing is for men to jump into the game and try something. The best way to learn to ride a bike is to get on it and try it. You may fall a few times and scrape a knee or two, but it is the only way to learn. Men can always change areas if it is not a good fit. You may want to arrange some easy, low-level opportunities for them to be exposed to various ministries. Through these they can see the ministry, ask questions, and try their hand at it. I like to have them start with smaller tasks and as they show themselves faithful, we add more responsibility (see Luke 16:10).

Teams. Most men have fond memories of being on a team. It may have been a Little League team, a high school team that won a conference title, or a work team that designed a new product. I have found it beneficial to approach ministry through teams. Let me mention a few advantages: You can get much more accomplished; there is more creativity; there is a sharing of the load and added accountability; there is help when you're getting tired; and there is synergy. So when you ask a man to serve, let him know he will not be alone; others who have been doing it for a while are able to help him get started. And when he takes a vacation or gets sick, they are there to cover for him and vice versa.

Equipping a Man for Service

Many men have a huge fear of failure. This can paralyze them if they feel they are not doing a job well. When they agree to serve, they also desire to succeed. Whether they verbalize it or not, they want training and ongoing support so they do not fail.

Training. When asking men to serve, there must be a willingness on the church's part to provide training. The principle we go by is, "Never ask a man to do anything you are not willing to train him for." So if you ask a man to lead a small group, it is important for him to have a healthy small-group experience as well as specific training as a group leader. This training can happen in many ways. For some it will be watching others and then joining them. For some, you might be able to provide training classes where they are given the basics and then allowed to practice in a safe environment. For others it may be by attending a seminar or reading a book. Or maybe it's a series of lessons they watch online and then discuss in a small group. Every ministry in your church should have training appropriate to the task and responsibility. Each of us will have to figure out how we can help them win in their area of service.

Ongoing support. It is one thing to get a man out of the pew and into the game; it is an entirely different thing to keep him in the game. Unfortunately, too many men in the church today have dipped their toe into service for a few weeks or months, but then fall back into taking up their normal parking spot and normal seat in the church. If we are going to encourage men to continue for the long term, there are some things we need to do. Everyone serving needs encouragement. They need to know you care and that they are doing a good job. You can encourage them through a verbal word, a written note, a quick e-mail, or a firm handshake. Most men I know have a pretty tough exterior, but inside they are tender and in need of encouragement. Let them know what they are doing is making a difference in the lives of those they are serving.

A second way to provide ongoing support is to continue to resource them with the tools necessary to do the ministry. There is nothing worse than trying to do a job and not having the tools to do it. If they are leading a small group, offer to buy a commentary on the book of the Bible they are studying. When you come across a good book or CD on leading small groups, pass it on to your leaders. I am constantly referring men to certain Web sites or books I have found helpful. For example, *Leadership Journal* has lots of beneficial articles on every subject under the sun. When a conference or seminar is in the area, encourage your men to attend for further training. Whether it is articles, books, CDs, DVDs, seminars, workshops, or Web sites, they all can let your leaders know how important they are and that you desire to help them develop into the person God wants them to be.

A third way to provide ongoing support is to stay connected with your men. No one serving in the ministry wants to feel like an island or feel they have been dumped on. Too often men step up to serve in the ministry, and with this huge burden lifted for us leaders, we forget about them! You may have never done this, but I sure have. One way to combat this is regular communication. Now, I am not talking daily or weekly. But when a person is first getting started, communicate with him regularly, and as time goes by and they feel more comfortable, you can back off a little. Our core leaders receive a monthly newsletter and I try to get together with them once a year to catch up, and this seems to work just fine. If something happens, they know I am available.

A final thing you can do is to keep the vision in front of them. The question men ask is, "Am I doing something worthwhile? Is it making any kingdom difference?" Our job as leaders is to remind them that what they are doing is worth it, that lives are being changed, and they are having an impact on eternity as a result. There are plenty of places they could be spending their time and money, and we need to ensure they understand the stakes and the contribution they are making.

So what is our job? Our job basically has four phases. We are forever praying, asking, training, and coaching men. If you do these things, you will discover as I have that there is no greater satisfaction than to see men discover their role, become involved, and leave their mark for eternity. Go to it.

RECOMMENDED READING

The Externally Focused Church by Rick Russaw and Eric Swanson

The Church of Irresistible Influence by Robert Lewis

The Volunteer Revolution by Bill Hybels

The New Reformation: Returning the Ministry to the People of God by Greg Ogden

S.H.A.P.E. by Erik Rees

Holy Discontent by Bill Hybels

Building Men Into Leaders

08

There is a dearth of good leadership in every segment of society today—in the business world, educational world, government, sports, and especially the church. Everywhere I go I am asked the same question, "How do you develop leaders for your ministry and church?"

These days I find myself spending more and more time building into emerging leaders, and there is nothing I would rather do more. Whether that is overseeing the intern program at Elmbrook, or spending two to four weeks overseas building into the 80 percent of pastors around the world who have no formal education, or meeting with dozens of men who are in various stages in their development as a leader.

For those of us who are leaders and working with men, I think you would have a hard time convincing us of anything more important. One of the greatest lessons I have learned in my ministry to men is that men desire to be leaders, but oftentimes they just don't know how. They are looking for all the help you can give them. I've learned that wise leaders invest themselves in the things that will have the greatest influence for the longest time. The development of leaders is perhaps the most lasting investment a leader can make, having an impact well beyond one's own lifespan. Bill Hybels, in *Courageous Leadership*, says, "You and I are at our leadership best when we provide challenging, soul-stirring kingdom opportunities for leaders in training; when we stand by these developing leaders and cheer them on; when we help them solve problems and pray for them; and when we coach them to higher levels of effectiveness. That's leadership at its best."[1] Without a conviction in our heart, it will never happen.

The greatest apologetic for developing leaders is found in Jesus himself. For the last year and a half of his life he invested in a small group of men who would become the leaders of the church. Our presence here today is proof that his leadership development process worked well. Guys, we need to develop leaders for the very same reason Jesus did; the future of the church depends on it.

Leadership Basics

You and I know that leaders do not fall from heaven; they are grown on earth in the context of the local church. If we are going to see a new generation of leaders in our church and ministry, we will need to be intentional and focused. I can tell you right now it will take time and effort, and your schedule will have to show it. Since I am responsible for leadership development at Elmbrook Church and spend a great amount of time in this area, I could probably write a book on the subject—but I'll stick with just a few key lessons I've learned over the last thirty years.

If you surveyed the church today, you would discover 101 programs for developing leaders. But the one principle I have learned more than any other is that the leadership culture is more important than the program. The proper culture allows for people to grow and develop. Here are a few of the aspects of an effective leadership culture.

Freedom to fail. Men need the freedom to take risks and do things they have not done before. Men by nature are entrepreneurs; they want to try new things. But too often in the church we micromanage them and do not give them the freedom to challenge the norm and take risks. One of the values we have at Elmbrook is if anything is worth doing, it is worth doing poorly. If men think they have to do everything perfectly, they will never step out and try new things. If you want to build an equipping ministry, you have to tear down the idol of excellence.

Principle of "looking." Every good leader is on the lookout for the next emerging leader. Leaders need to have their eyes open to identify and invite others into ministry. Every time my leadership team gets together I ask the same question: "Who are you seeing that might be a potential leader?" When I get together with a small-group leader, I ask them the same question. In a conversation with a vice president of Harley-Davidson Motorcycle Company a few years ago, I asked him how they keep a constant flow of leaders. He said, "We are forever looking for the next thirty-six leaders. Every meeting starts with the question, 'Who are we going to invite and invest in?'"

Principle of "with." Leaders are always looking for an opportunity to take newer leaders with them when doing ministry. Not only do they see the ministry being modeled by you, but the travel time allows for many deep and meaningful conversations. So whether you are leading a Bible study, visiting someone in the hospital, or speaking at a retreat, think of taking another man with you to enhance their development. You cannot impact lives from a distance; young emerging leaders need proximity to real leaders.

Resources. A culture should be fostered where all leaders have the resources needed to grow, develop, and do the ministry. I am constantly resourcing our leaders with books, articles, CDs, Web sites, blogs, seminars, conferences, and other material that will help them grow. Years ago I heard Rick Warren say, "When a leader stops learning, he stops leading." I have lived by that principle in my own life and have fostered it in the leaders I work with as well. Every leader learns in a different way. Some more by audio, some visual, and some need to talk it out. As a leader of men you will have to help them discover how they best learn and then put them in a situation where they can leverage it.

Care, love, and encouragement. Every leader needs to feel they are a better person because they are in leadership at your church. They need to feel cared for, appreciated, and encouraged in what they are doing. When leaders have been around for a while it is easy to take them for granted. A culture of development treats every leader with dignity, respect, and value.

The "sweet spot" principle. There is absolutely nothing more frustrating than to be serving and leading in an area that is not consistent with how God wired you. In the very same way as a football coach, I continually seek to get the players in the right position to maximize their talent to the fullest. The goal is for every leader to be serving in their passion/gift area. Part of leadership development is to help them know their capacity, strengths, and weaknesses.

A culture of renewal. Provide opportunity for leaders to hit the Pause button and experience Sabbath and the renewal of their soul. This will mean providing soul care for your leaders. One of the biggest problems we see with leaders is burnout. They are working fifty to sixty hours a week on their job, pouring into their families, and carrying huge loads at church. I have found it extremely important to help the men develop a schedule that is sustainable for the long run. For example, I will regularly meet with a man to go over his weekly and monthly schedule to help him prioritize the things he is doing or should be doing. Oftentimes there is no time for devotions or rest or exercise. Just recently I asked a leader to take a year off of ministry to spend more time with his family and to replenish his soul. Boy, was he surprised by that suggestion!

Reward equippers over the doers. In a culture of people development, those who get rewarded are not the ones who do things but those who empower other people to do things. They see it as their role to equip other people. One of the chief responsibilities of a leader is to equip others to do the work of the ministry (Ephesians 4:11–12). Therefore, in our development process we are constantly helping the leaders catch a vision for developing others.

Develop leaders, not use leaders. I saved this for last on purpose. I believe it is the biggest trap we fall into as ministry leaders. Too often our training is for the purpose of simply keeping the church machine going rather than developing people to lead the ministries that will change the world. Therefore, when people are tired or burned out, we simply let them go rather than build into them. Our goal is to help every leader become what God wants them to be and do. This may mean helping them find a place of leadership in another ministry.

Having a kingdom mentality will be extremely beneficial for this to happen.

As you can see, I have not spoken much about the actual how-tos of developing leaders; I wanted to paint a picture of what the right environment would look and feel like for young emerging leaders to blossom. Take some time right now to evaluate your present leadership culture and see what needs to be changed or developed.

Exercise—Leadership Culture

1. Let each person share how they developed as a leader.

   Was there someone who saw potential in you and asked you to grow it?

   Was there someone who invested time and energy in you?

   What were some of the initial responsibilities given to you?

   When did you first know you had some leadership abilities?

2. What words would best describe the leadership culture of your ministry or church?

3. What is healthy about the culture and what is unhealthy?

4. How would you envision creating a better culture for development to take place?

Leadership Development Is a Process

A second lesson learned over the years is that leadership development is a process more than it is a program. So often we want to get men into the right program or have them read the right book or attend the right conference, and then somehow they will become leaders. Not that any of the above are wrong in and of themselves, but there is so much more to it. For the process to work it needs to be personal, slow, holistic, and intentional. To be personal means that one size does not fit all when it comes to developing people. Every man you work with comes from a different background, with different experiences, relationships, maturity level, giftedness, and passions. These all have to be taken into consideration when putting together a plan for him.

In my initial meeting with a man, I will ask as many questions as possible to find out where he has been, where he is presently, and where he wants to go. Some of the questions I will ask are:

- Share with me your journey of faith.

- What experiences in life have shaped you the most?

- What people have had the greatest influence on your life?

- What leadership experiences have you had in the past?

- What would other people say you do well? Not so well?

- What are your passions? What kingdom assignment/adventure gets you the most excited?

- Where do you want to grow as a leader? How can we help you?

- Where do you see yourself five years from now?

These types of questions begin to give me an idea of where they are and where they want to grow and go in the future. With this in mind we can begin to put together a plan that is personalized for them. For example, if they want to learn how to study Scripture better, we can get them into a class to help them. If they are weak on theology, they can take a Study Center course. If they want to learn how to lead a small group, we can match them up as an apprentice with a veteran leader. Of course the problem is it can get a bit messy with men at different places and doing different things.

Second, the process will be slow. The two myths we must overcome are that leaders can be mass produced in large quantities, and that they can be microwaved quickly. As I mentioned back in the chapter on discipleship, one of the key findings during my study on leadership development was that churches that were doing a good job of developing leaders for the kingdom were churches that had an intentional discipleship plan. The church-wide discipleship process served as the basis for the leadership development they were doing. So in our case, we had to take a step back as a church and lay this foundation of discipleship before we could add the leadership development pieces. There will be some men in your church who have never been discipled and are lacking some of the essentials in their lives. It could take a year or so to lay a foundation, but once they have it down, you can start addressing the leadership issues. If you are growing small-group leaders and someone has shown interest and aptitude for this area, you will want to get them into a group as an apprentice leader, where they can learn from the main leader. As time goes on, the leader can give them more and more responsibility, per Luke 16:10.

In the midst of this you can also encourage participating in any small-group leader training your church may offer. This training will only make sense if they are actually in a small-group situation. When ready, the young leader can be given a group of their own, with a shepherd to walk alongside him. One of the biggest problems we have run into is the men who think they have "arrived" when they become a small-group leader. They think they know it all, but I continually remind our leaders that no matter what their position, they need to keep learning and growing. So continue to check in with new small-group leaders, and ask what they are learning about leadership, shepherding, and ministering to men. Continue to resource them with materials to help them grow and develop.

There may be some small-group leaders who become shepherds over a number of groups, and others who are invited to join the small-group leadership team and become coordinators. I hope you have seen the principle here. It is slow and it is progressive. All along the line men are given more and more responsibility based on maturity, capacity, and how well they work in the areas given to them. Looking back I can see that for most men, this process of growing into vital leaders takes several years, and it is a process that cannot be hurried.

Third, the process is holistic. In order for a man to develop, you must look at the total man. For this reason, I am constantly thinking about the following areas of a man's life and his development in each:

- Character formation—the being. This is best done in the context of a small group where a man can talk about life below the surface and be held accountable for his actions, attitudes, and words (we'll look into this further). In Christian leadership there is nothing more important than character, and there is nothing that takes longer to develop than a man's character.

- Competency training—the doing. This can be done through a small group or through special classes, seminars, and conferences. But there is nothing better than giving a man real-life experiences to speed up the process and opportunity to refine his skills. Some of the skills they will need to develop over the years are team building, recruiting, vision-casting, coaching, spiritual formation, communicating, mobilizing others, resourcing your ministry, and how to facilitate a small group.

- Cognitive training—the knowing. In order to lead, a man must have a Christian worldview. He must know what he believes and why he believes it. This should be covered in the basic discipleship process, but if not, it will need to be developed here. For some guys this will be a basic theology course, for others a worldview class or going through something like the Truth Project or Chuck Colson's book *How Now Shall We Live?*

- Calling clarification—the what. Most men I have worked with have never gone through the process of truly understanding how God made them and what their purpose is in life. For years now I have been using material by Church Resource Ministry (www.crmnet.org) entitled *Focusing Your Life and Ministry,* and the men have found it extremely helpful. The basic principle is that our future is anchored in our past and God has put us through various experiences, situations, and relationships to prepare us for the future. The calling clarification segment is necessary to help a man find his sweet spot in leadership.

- Chemistry issues—with whom. Men by nature are independent and isolated from one another and oftentimes do not work well with others. Part of the development process is to get them on a team and learn what it is to check their pride at the door, handle conflict, and learn teamwork. Then they are ready to lead a team. They may have all the talent in the world, but if they are unable to get along with others, it can all go to waste.

- Communion developed—with him. The leaders' work will only be as strong and effective as their walk with Jesus. Too often in our development of leaders we ignore the heart and what God is doing there. In everything we do we are constantly talking about the spiritual disciplines and what it means to fall more and more in love with Jesus and his people.

Finally, building leaders needs to be intentional. I like to refer to it as the leadership pipeline. Sometimes when men first become involved in church and ministry they tend to be like crude oil—not very useful. There are lots of wounds, struggles, sin areas, lack of commitment, fledgling faith, etc. I have found it very helpful to have a general plan for men to follow that covers the basics but also allows for it to be personal. Along the way we have established various refining stations that build into their lives the various topics we just covered. For example, our discipleship course for men, Basic Training, covers How to Study the Bible, Evangelism, Servant Leadership, Being a Godly Father and Husband, Christianity, and Work. As the men progress through the thirty-two-week study with eleven other men, each of these modules serves as refining stations. Upon completion, he is ready for some additional training in the area of leadership. I will also lead studies on calling, small-group leading, leadership essentials, and other various topics that help get the men to where they want to be.

Everything I have just mentioned has not been randomly thrown out there, but has come about after much prayer and discussion, thinking through what we want the men to look like and be able to do when they come out of the pipeline.

The Leadership Pipeline

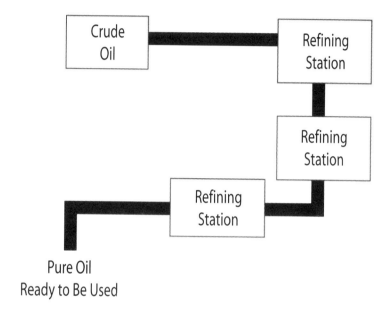

Exercise—Leadership Process

1. Describe what you are presently doing to develop leaders for your church and ministry.

2. How intentional are you being in your development of new leaders?

3. Do a quick evaluation of how you are doing in each of these areas.

	Poor		OK		Excellent
Character—the "being"	1	2	3	4	5
Competency—the "doing"	1	2	3	4	5
Cognitive—the "knowing"	1	2	3	4	5
Calling—the "what"	1	2	3	4	5
Chemistry—the "with whom"	1	2	3	4	5
Communion—the "with him"	1	2	3	4	5

4. What do you see as being some key "refining stations" for the men of your church/ministry?

5. What steps must you take to develop a comprehensive plan that is progressive in nature?

Leadership Development Groups

As we have seen, leaders do not fall from heaven; they are grown on earth in the context of the local church. To be effective we must be intentional and focused. Let me present one way I have developed leaders for the ministry, and for the church as a whole.

I believe the development of leaders happens best in small groups, and that is why we call these groups Leadership Development Groups. Over the past several years I have led a number of these types of groups for men from all different backgrounds and ministries. I normally like to have ten to twelve men in the group, and we meet weekly for six to nine months. Now, the natural question that comes up is, Who do you choose to be in the group? Great question; I'm glad you asked. Here are a few principles I keep in mind when inviting men to join me:

- We have discovered most of the leaders are already in the church, they just need to be asked and developed.

- The men will have been through our church's discipleship process to ensure we are all on the same page.

- The men will have been serving in a ministry for a couple of years. I don't want men who have just gone through the discipleship process and don't have ministry experience.

- The men have demonstrated some leadership potential, have a desire to learn and grow, and are available to meet.

- The men have shown themselves to be godly men who are seeking to submit their entire being to Jesus and live a life powered by the Holy Spirit.

The group time is usually divided into two components. The first is small-group time with three to four men in a group. They are usually in these groups for thirty to forty-five minutes each week. It is during this time where they deal with the character and relationship issues in their lives. They share their lives, hold each other accountable, and pray for one another. It is here they see what a biblically functioning group looks like. They may not realize it, but what I am seeking to do is give them a healthy small-group experience they can replicate.

The second half of the meeting is spent in a large group, looking at a number of leadership issues related to the pipeline and what we are seeking to develop. I usually spend the first six to eight weeks dealing with the calling issue. For this I walk them through the material developed by Church Resource Ministry called *Focusing Your Life and Ministry*. While doing this we read Os Guinness's book *The Call*. For one of the sessions I'll have them watch Bill Hybels's session from the Leadership Summit on Holy Discontent. All of this helps them get a sense for how God made them and what the mission is that he has for their lives. By the end they have developed a personal mission statement and a set of life values.

At the end of this section, each of the men give a ten-minute report to the rest of the group on what they discovered through the process. It is easily one of the most gratifying times of the year for me.

We then move on to discuss some of the competencies needed to be an effective leader. For this we walk chapter by chapter through the book of Nehemiah. This book covers such topics as the personal life of a leader, prayer and the leader, planning your ministry, casting vision, recruiting, handling conflict, dealing with temptation as a leader, resourcing your ministry, and a host of other issues. Throughout the study the men are given various experiential exercises to complete that correspond to the topic of the day.

Along with this we walk through *Spiritual Leadership* by Henry Blackaby. The final component of the process is for each man to do an independent study on whatever aspect of leadership they want to study in-depth. They spend a number of weeks interviewing people, researching, and then they make a presentation to the group on what they have discovered. Again, because it is personal, they usually get really excited about it and everyone benefits.

Now, I am not saying you have to do it this way. What I can say is after seventeen years of leading these classes, the number of men we have sent off to ministries all over the church, community, and world is staggering. There is something about developing leaders in small groups that is very different from one-on-one teaching. I am convinced it is the most important thing I do as a pastor. So where do you start? Start praying right now for twelve men whom God would want you to build into next year, and then start looking for the divine appointments to ask them.

There are a couple of other resources you may want to look at for this small-group experience.

1. *Joshua's Men* by Injoy—A twelve-month experience where you meet with twelve men once a month for four hours. I have looked over the material and talked with several pastors who have used it, and they have nothing but positive things to say.

2. *Leadership Essentials* by Greg Ogden—This workbook is a follow-up to *Discipleship Essentials*. It covers many of the subjects

mentioned above. There is a weekly Bible study, a reading, and an exercise to encourage deeper thinking.

Exercise—Small-Group Leadership

1. What is going to be the criteria for inviting men to join the small-group experience?

2. What do we want this experience to look like?

What are some experiences we want them to have?

What is the desired outcome?

What are some materials we can walk through together?

What will the modules be?

Who is going to lead it?

When do we want to start? How long will it be? When will it meet?

Learn by Doing

There is absolutely no substitute for giving men a kingdom responsibility. In the same way you cannot learn to swim in a classroom, you cannot learn to lead in the classroom either. My guess is each of you can look back at one person who gave you your first kingdom responsibility, and if you were like me, you had no idea what you were doing, but they entrusted it to you anyway.

I owe a huge thank-you to Tim Ryder, who was the high school pastor at Elmbrook back in the late seventies. I had just moved back home after my freshman year of college, and I had been attending a small Bible study at the high school. But the leader had gotten the call to go to seminary, so the group was without a leader. When Tim heard I was back in town, he called me and asked to get together. When we met he told me of the need for a person to lead the study at Brookfield Central. I told him I had been a Christian for less than two years and had no idea what to do with a group. I had never spoken to a group before, never led a Bible study, never organized a ministry or even discipled or counseled a student! His response was "So what! There is a need, you are available, now get to it." He reminded me of the age-old principle that God will never call us to do anything he is unwilling to equip us to do.

I showed up at the first meeting and had absolutely no idea what to do with the fifteen students. After the singing and announcements I spoke for almost an hour, until some of the students just got up and started to leave! Not a real strong confirmation I was doing the right thing. After the rough start, Tim continued to meet with me on a regular basis for the next five years to encourage me, coach me, and train me. Five leaders later we had over 150 students meeting on a weekly basis in the basements of homes all over the community. Through the experience I learned how to prepare and give messages, recruit college-age leaders, delegate responsibilities to the students, and raise money for the ministry, and in the end I sensed God's calling me to ministry. None of this would have happened if Tim would not have asked me to just get into the game. The lessons learned could not be learned in a classroom but rather by rolling up my spiritual sleeves and getting dirty.

It is no different for the men in your church and ministry. The only way they will learn leadership lessons is if you entrust them with some kingdom responsibilities. One of the experiences we like to give young leaders is to put them on a ministry team where they will be working with several other high-octane leaders. I love the team approach to leadership development for several reasons.

1. Leadership is being modeled for them by others.
2. There is someone to watch them, encourage them, and work with them.
3. There is built-in accountability for what they are doing.
4. As a leadership team, we can get constant feedback on who is progressing and showing themselves faithful in the little things, so we can entrust them with more.

A great example of this is Mike, a young man we asked to be on the No Regrets Men's Conference team over ten years ago. During his first year he simply helped one of the team members with registration. The second year we asked him to head up that area, the third year we asked him to co-coordinate the conference, and the next year we asked him to coordinate the entire conference. Today Mike is one of the finest leaders we have in the church. He heads up a team of eighteen men who run a conference for seven thousand men in four different sites around the state. Through the process he has learned how to cast vision, recruit team members, delegate responsibility, and perform numerous other leadership skills. I am so proud of the way he has grown and taken his kingdom responsibility seriously. He will never know the thousands of men's lives that have been touched by his ministry.

Often I am asked how much training is required before a man can start leading an area. Usually the men have been involved in one way or another before they start leading, so the first training is giving them a healthy small-group or team experience. Our general policy is to orientate them, involve them in doing it, and then train them. Too often in this country we over-train our people. I am much more a proponent of the ready-fire-aim philosophy than the more common ready-aim-fire philosophy. With a little experience under their belt, the training is so much more meaningful than just theory.

The bottom line is rather simple: People learn best when they are doing it, not just talking about it and watching. For our leadership development to have any teeth to it, it must involve their getting out of the pews and into the game.

Exercise—Learn by Doing

1. Who are some men that you need to give a ministry experience to?

2. What are some experiences that you can entrust men with?

3. What are some ministry teams that are ready for a man or two to join?

Leadership Development Involves Coaching

The final area I want to touch on is the topic of coaching. I have found it is one thing to recruit, train, and delegate an area of ministry to a highly capable person, but it is an entirely different thing to stay connected to him and to see him as a lifelong learner. I have a tendency to neglect them once they start leading. What I am learning is that once they are serving in the right area, my job is to help them continue to grow and develop, and this is where coaching comes in.

As the ministry develops, you will need to have other key leaders who are coaches as well, as there will be too many leaders for you to handle them all. I find my key coaching roles to be with my key coordinators, who in turn are coaching the men on their ministry teams. One of the first things I learned about coaching is that it is different for every man. There are some who have been leading small groups for seventeen years and they really are not interested in getting together on a regular basis. Others would like to meet weekly, and there is everything in between. I normally take my cue from the men as to what they need and are looking for.

There are generally three components to my coaching meetings, which are normally over breakfast or lunch. One of the most helpful books for me and all of our coaches is *Coaching 101* by Bobby Logan. In the book he says there are three components of a good coaching meeting. First, there is a time of reflection. This is an opportunity to look back at the ministry and their life and to see how things are going for them. What have they learned, experienced, and dealt with as a leader? This could be something about parenting or shepherding someone who has lost their job, or new insight on recruiting potential leaders. During the discussion I want to make sure they are learning from the pain or lessons; I want them to understand that they have never arrived—that they can always be learning and growing. Sometimes we will read a book together about a subject they want to grow in. When we get together we will discuss the main points of the book and lessons learned and applied.

The second part of the meeting has to do with refocusing. This is looking forward to what lies ahead. Where are they going with the ministry, what leaders will they need, where do they want to grow, what challenges are they facing at home, at work, in the ministry?

The third component of the meeting is the resource segment. What resources will they need to make this happen? What do they need from a budget perspective, leader resources, support, and encouragement from the church or ministry? Is there any new training they will need to be better equipped for the responsibilities they have or will have? Again, the meeting is made up of three components: a time to reflect, refocus, and look at resources.

When it comes to coaching, there are a few skills I have developed over time and found to be very beneficial.

1. *The art of listening.* A coaching session is not a time to lecture or teach, but rather a time to listen. As a leader they are giving and giving and they need a safe place they can vent and not be judged or condemned. There has been many a time when I just wanted to unload all this good information on them but had to bite my tongue and listen to what was going on in their lives, family, and ministry. There is no substitute for listening.

2. *The art of asking good questions.* This goes hand in hand with listening. Coaches are forever making lists of good questions to ask and looking for open nerves in the leaders' lives. When you hear them speak of pain, hurt, confusion, or uncertainty, it is time to ask more penetrating questions to get at the issue. You may want to start making a list of potential questions at the end of this chapter to use in coaching settings.

3. *Prayerful preparation.* I never go into one of these meetings without praying for the leader and for our time together. Both of us have many other things we could be doing, and I want to make sure God uses this time for his glory. I pray that God would give me ears to hear what is really going on in his life, to be able to ask questions that open him up and get to the real issues, and to say the right things in the right way to him. I always finish the time with the leader by asking how I can pray for him until we meet again.

4. *Always one more thing.* When in a coaching relationship, I am always thinking of what is next for that leader. What is the next growth area for him personally, spiritually, leadership-wise? I never want leaders to get stagnant and feel like they have arrived.

Building Men Into Leaders • 119

5. *One thing at a time.* When working with leaders, I do not want to overwhelm them with too many things to work on at once. I'd rather give them one thing to work on until we meet again. It may be trying to encourage their wife on a more regular basis, having devotions more regularly, or learning to listen to their team better. Whatever it is, I try to keep it to one item at a time.

6. *Invest in your men.* It takes a leader to develop a leader. Emerging leaders need proximity and closeness to the real deal. I will say it one more time: The closer you get to the men, the greater impact you will have.

Guys, in some ways it is very simple. Identify potential leaders, invest your life and time in them, and give them some responsibility and let them go. Having spent the better part of my life doing just that, I can tell you there is no greater joy, no greater sense of satisfaction, no greater investment than investing in young leaders who will carry the torch of leadership long after we are gone.

Exercise—Coaching

1. Who are the men in your ministry that need to be coached?

2. Who are some men that could help you with the coaching responsibilities?

3. What are some questions you could ask in a coaching session?
   Reflection Questions:

   Refocusing Questions:

   Resource Questions:

Recommended Reading

The Training of the Twelve by A. B. Bruce

The Master Plan of Evangelism by Robert Coleman

Transforming Leadership by Leighton Ford

Leaders on Leaders by George Barna

The Making of a Leader by Robert Clinton

Developing Leaders Around You by John Maxwell

Everyone's a Coach by Don Shula and Ken Blanchard

Coaching 101 by Robert Logan

Mentoring Leaders by Carson Pue

NOTES

1. Bill Hybels, *Courageous Leadership* (Grand Rapids: Zondervan, 2002), 135.

MINISTERING TO TWENTYSOMETHING MEN

09

No one ministering in the church today can avoid noticing that we have a new breed in our midst. These young adults deserve close inspection and understanding if we are going to have an effective ministry to them. Maybe you've been involved in men's ministry for years but you and your church are struggling to reach men in their twenties. Or maybe you've recently tried to share your faith with a younger co-worker and you're wondering why your approach doesn't seem to work. Do you know a post-college-age man who has wandered from the faith and you'd love to help him reconnect with God but don't know where to begin? Don't feel bad; you're not alone. I hear it all the time: "How do you reach and minister to twentysomething men?"

I don't have all the answers, but we have definitely learned a great deal and tried a number of things over the years. Some things have worked and some have bombed! In this chapter I will draw on my own experience, but better than that, the experience of one of my younger brothers, Brian, who was the twentysomething pastor at Elmbrook for five years before planting an urban church in downtown Milwaukee to reach even more young adults.

For years I would have Brian do a seminar at our men's training conference on ministering to men in their twenties, and it was always the most popular and best attended. For the past eight years he has learned much about ministry to men in their twenties, but he also has experience . . .

he is a Gen Xer himself. So the lessons learned are of his friends, some of whom have come to know Christ personally and are passionately following him. Many others are still on their journey and desperately need to hear a story greater than their own individual stories. I will start by helping you understand this new generation of men and then provide some practical applications for you and your ministry to them. I have also listed a number of books that are helpful on the subject. So let's get started.

The following passage of Scripture has become very important to me as I minister to people of the next generation.

> O my people, listen to my instructions. Open your ears to what I am saying, for I will speak to you in a parable. I will teach you hidden lessons from our past—stories we have heard and known, stories our ancestors handed down to us. We will not hide these truths from our children; we will tell the next generation about the glorious deeds of the Lord, about his power and his mighty wonders. For he issued his laws to Jacob; he gave his instructions to Israel. He commanded our ancestors to teach them to their children, so the next generation might know them—even the children not yet born—and they in turn will teach their own children. So each generation should set its hope anew on God, not forgetting his glorious miracles and obeying his commands.
>
> PSALM 78:1–7 (NLT)

God has commanded every generation to pass the truth about himself ("The Story") to each succeeding generation so that it can become their story too. But sometimes we need to revisit the ways in which we pass on this great message. The message does not change—it is timeless. But the means by which we share it may change, culture by culture, person to person, and it is not different with this generation of people.

As you may know, twentysomethings are part of what is known as Generation Y or the Millennials. This generation includes people born roughly between 1975 and 1995. They make up a whopping 25 percent of our population, or 70 million men and women.

No matter how you slice this generation, it's more about attitude than age. I know people in their 40s and 50s, technically baby boomers, who fully identify with the attitudes and tone of Generation Y. In fact, you may find yourself reading the description of Gen Y and saying, "Wow, that describes me!"

Understanding this generation means getting close enough to meet real men with real stories to share. When you listen to their stories, you hear some common elements. I've identified four forces that have shaped a generation.

1. Postmodernism

Many men in their twenties have a postmodern worldview. Josh McDowell and Bob Hostetler offer this definition of postmodernism: "A worldview characterized by the belief that truth doesn't exist in any objective sense but is created rather than discovered." Truth is "created by the specific culture and exists only in that culture. Therefore, any system or statement that tries to communicate truth is a power play, an effort to dominate other cultures."[1] The following lists help describe the differences:

Modernism	Postmodernism
Truth	Preference
Autonomous self	Community
Scientific discovery	Virtual reality
Human progress	Human misery
Head leads heart	Heart leads head
Star Trek	*The Matrix*

Postmodernists tend to filter truth and approach life subjectively. The implication, then, for ministry to them is that we will have a difficult time persuading them that Christianity is the only serious option for a successful life. Of course, this doesn't mean they are a lost cause. In fact, one-on-one ministry is ideal for twentysomethings.

Postmodernists doubt the validity of one central story covering all people and all history. But they are very open to personal stories. Stories give meaning to the lives of individuals. When working with a guy in his twenties, it helps to emphasize living the truth up close versus talking, lecturing, and teaching the truth from a distance. This applies to both evangelism and discipleship. A personal approach to ministry has always been God's way, but perhaps never more vital than now.

2. Broken and Blended Families

Forty percent of the young adults of Generation Y come from homes broken by divorce. The concept of the latchkey kid exploded with this generation. When you put together the number of children who come from divorce and were latchkey kids, you have a generation of young adults who have been alone more than any generation in history. Many grew up in a day care and spent hours watching MTV and playing video games. For this generation, holidays and other typical family gatherings aren't always joyful. Fatherless and latchkey kids, it turns out, crave community but suffer from the socially debilitating effects of shame, alienation, and loneliness.

Brian told me of a recent conversation with a small group of twenty-somethings in his ministry. He asked each to share about one "good" marriage they had seen in their lifetime. Of the six, only one man had seen a "good" model of marriage. Two men had witnessed their parents marry and divorce multiple times. And sadly, two men shared of Christian parents who stayed married but have lived in separate bedrooms for years.

To minister to men so accustomed to brokenness, we must sincerely value relationship. If you can model what healthy friendship and marriage look like, you can disciple this generation!

Trust will not come easily to the men of this generation. Be prepared for initial skepticism or cynicism to color their reaction to the gospel. Fears of abandonment run high; we need to keep our promises.

Gen Y is longing for real community. We can provide that. As the fatherless men of this generation struggle to understand their masculinity, we need to provide honest teaching on sexuality and model strong male friendship. Mentor couples are also needed in their lives to show that lifelong marriage can work.

3. The Digital Economy

Generation Y is the first truly electronic generation. They were raised and continue to live fully "at home" with cell phones, pagers, Palm Pilots, iPhones, texting, Facebook, the Internet, and, of course, e-mail. These are not people who are intimidated by new technology.

This group sees their economic prospects on two levels: as individuals, they express hope and confidence, but as a group, they have far less hope for a secure long-term future.

Interestingly, this group (aged twenty-five to thirty-four) is three times more likely to start their own business than the thirty-five- to fifty-five-year-olds. Yet, these are not men who live for their jobs. Gen Yers perceive little loyalty from employers and show little in return. They change jobs often. They work to live—love a challenge—but don't want to miss out on things that involve family and friends. They do not want to make the same mistakes their fathers made of making work a god to be worshiped and the place that takes them away from their family.

As for spending habits, young men buy things because they think they deserve them. The previous generation bought things because they thought they earned it. Gen Y buys what they want when they want it because they are afraid it won't be around if they wait until they can afford it.

As you minister to these men, you must acknowledge the economic uncertainties they face. However, seek to instill hope. They may be cynical or suspicious regarding how the church as an "institution" spends its money, but if they are committed to something personally, they will give wholeheartedly and generously. As part of my mentoring relationship, I bring up the issue of personal finances as a matter of discipleship. If a young man is struggling financially, sometimes the most Christian thing to do is to help him create a working budget!

4. Popular Culture

It seems that this is the first generation of which it can be said that their primary (for many, their *only*) frame of cultural reference is pop culture. The TV served as a surrogate parent for many of these kids. One survey found the average Gen Y watched eighty-nine movies each year, equaling 1.7 per week (usually DVDs), and 67 percent said that music played an essential role in their daily lives. Media, in all its vast presence, offers an escape route from everyday life that they are accustomed to taking. Harry Potter is their Peter Pan.

Having digested the message "image is everything," this generation has concluded, to some serious degree, that everything is merely image, insubstantial, unreal. We must offer the truth. The gospel is a substantial rock of truth on which all generations can stand. As mentors to this generation, integrity, vulnerability, and authenticity will be demanded of us. If our faith is substantial and real then they will find hope for their own journey of faith.

It is a misrepresentation of Generation Y to say they have short attention spans. This is an age group that wants many answers to many questions and all in a hurry; there is a lot to learn! In general, they are voracious learners who love to sort through massive amounts of information at a very fast pace. To attract and hold their interest we must consider the wise and creative use of media in our ministry planning. And it isn't just a good idea, but it is mandatory that you change formats and procedures within the ministry to honor their eclectic style. In so doing, we validate the discussion about pop culture just like every area of life. Generation Y needs to be taught to evaluate popular culture from a Christian worldview.

At least once a year, Brian's ministry did a series of messages that explored significant spiritual themes in contemporary movies. Obviously this requires discernment in today's culture, but it can also provide an important connecting point for ministry to this generation. You may want to consider forming a men's movie group to watch quality films and then go out afterward to discuss its relation to Christian faith.

Discipling a New Generation

With this as a backdrop, allow me to share some key principles for your work with this exciting generation. One of the most rewarding aspects of the last couple of years has been to see a number of young men commit their life to Christ, to take serious the call to follow hard after Jesus and step up to the plate and serve Christ here in the church and in the community.

1. *A new way of looking at discipleship.* As you walk alongside the men of Generation Y, consider that you may need to adjust your road map of the journey. The modern model for the process of discipleship is giving way to the postmodern model that you see when you hear their stories.

If you have been a Christian for a number of years, your conversion most likely fits the "modern" process. If you weren't raised in a Christian home, at some point you had contact with a Christian who explained the gospel. You eventually made a commitment to Christ and continued the journey of growth. Your journey eventually brought you to the church—a community of believers—which you embraced, knowing it would be necessary for your spiritual growth. Before Generation Y, there was typically a sharp definition between evangelism and discipleship.

Today the lines between evangelism and discipleship blur. Gen Yers will often commit to Christian community before they have committed their lives to Christ. They don't need to be convinced about the value of building friendships with others. They crave community. And as they experience authentic Christian community, they learn what it means to be a Christ follower. When they finally cross the line of faith, they may discover that they have been "discipled" along the way and didn't even realize it! That's Jeremy's story. He attended church very infrequently growing up and stopped entirely once he got to college. But Jeremy never stopped believing in God. Soon after starting his career as an engineer, a Christian friend invited him to one of our ministry small-group Bible studies. He absolutely loved it. "The people were so real," he recalled. "The relationships I built in those few months were deeper than the friendships I've had since junior high. I know now it's because God was a part of it all." Jeremy was experiencing genuine biblical community. He came faithfully every week to the group for two years. He listened. He participated. And he asked lots of questions just like everyone else in the group. After two years of being a member of the Christian community, Jeremy put his faith in Christ as his Lord and Savior. Jeremy's "only" been a Christian for six months, but he has been discipled now for two years, and currently he is discipling some college-age guys who are wandering just like he once was.

2. *Making it work.* The Gen Y disciple is ready and willing to integrate faith and works. Your job in discipleship is to help them integrate the content of Christianity into real-life situations. Brian tells the story of taking a guy to a popular movie. Afterward, they sat down over coffee for a couple of hours and discussed how the movie related to their lives. Who knew ministry could be so fun? What we have discovered is that if we are going to effectively minister to these young men, we need to understand the life stage they are in and the issues that go with that stage. For many men under thirty-five, there are three key issues on their minds: getting married, growing their career, and having children. As a result, they want training that will help them to grow in these three areas. Each year we offer three classes for young dads. They are "I'm a Dad, Now What?" "She Calls Me Daddy," and "Raising a Modern-Day Knight." These have been extremely popular among the younger dads, and they are a great way to introduce them to small groups. These guys are not just interested in theory, they want to know how to practically work things out in life.

3. *Mobilize to serve.* Twentysomethings have hearts as big as basketballs, and they want to use their time and resources to better the community and world. Whether it is starting a non-governmental organization to bring clean water to Nigeria, teaching English as a second language in the Congo, or pounding nails for Habitat for Humanity, these men's hearts are full of compassion for those less fortunate. One key way to help them grow in their discipleship is to mobilize them for service. They do not want to watch; they want to participate. The more opportunities you can give them across the street and around the world the better. Spend some time together in some form of service to the needy and discuss Christian compassion, or after working together on a community clean-up project discuss Christian stewardship of the environment.

I love short-term mission projects because they help connect the head, the heart, and the hands in the Christian faith. But remember, you don't need to go overseas to integrate faith and real life. Clearly the possibilities are many. The point is to value community and relationship, not as separate from or secondary to biblical teaching, but as integral with teaching.

4. *Model it.* Young men are tired of the talk. They want to see it being lived out in your life. The greatest rap against older generations is their hypocrisy. These guys grew up watching their parents go to church yet get divorced and act no different from everyone else. They can spot a fake a mile away, so if we are going to have an impact in their lives, we must be authentic and real. For example, Generation Y has already embraced the ancient spiritual disciplines of solitude, fasting, sacrificial giving, journaling, meditation, and prayer. They accept these practices but need direction on how to make them a part of authentic Christian discipleship. Are you comfortable being scrutinized personally regarding your integration of these practices in your journey of faith? This is how this generation will grow into tomorrow's leadership. They will "buy into" you, not your leadership. Offering guidance within the context of a real relationship is how you will be an effective mentor today.

To this generation, your personal model as a disciple maker is more important than any other teaching. Do you value people and make commitments of integrity? Allow yourself to become important to someone of this generation; seek out a role in their life as spiritual mentor. Most Gen Yers lack the trust to pursue you as their mentor, but they will respond if asked.

Expect discipleship to take time. This is a generation with more brokenness and less Christian background than ever before. With patience you can help them see how their story fits into God's Great Story. Your encouragement will draw them into the embrace of the family of God. You will be an agent to show them how they are gifted for service to the body and how their passions and deep longings can flourish as they exercise their gifts. Offer practical training and opportunities for service and de-emphasize teaching a set of doctrines to be memorized.

The men of this generation are risk-takers, and they are willing to go anywhere and do anything in the name of Jesus. When I hear about what they are doing and where they are taking the gospel, it puts me to shame. How we can help is to get behind their ideas and let them fly.

The men of Generation Y are prepared for their lives to be changed, knowing that words like *open, honest,* and *vulnerable* are key to growth. But they will want you to go first. If you sense they are hiding behind a mask, they probably are. Are you? If so, go first and live vulnerably. I find when my teaching is filled *only* with positive examples from my life, very few people come up to talk with me afterward. But when I share a struggle from my life or marriage and testify to God's grace and power, people are literally standing in line to share their stories. Admitting the hard truths about yourself will develop the foundation of respect required for your Gen Y disciple to admit his mistakes and grow. Provide the safe environment where truth can be tested and faith stretched, both yours and theirs.

5. *Go to them.* One of the things we have learned is that our men's ministry is perceived as "my dad's ministry," not theirs! We realize that most Gen Y guys are not going to attend a GameDay Breakfast on Saturday morning, nor are they going to go on a retreat with a bunch of "old" guys. We have decided to go to them and do ministry on their turf rather than ours. This means we have asked some men's leaders to get involved in the college-age ministry and the twentysomething ministry. Rob, a good friend of mine, went to the twentysomething ministry and found six guys who wanted to be in a small group, and he has been leading them for the past six months. He takes the principles he has learned in our ministry and applies them to these men. For example, they were not interested in working through our regular discipleship manual, but they were interested in talking about each of the topics in the manual. They are not into programs, but rather relationships. Rob has learned to spend a great deal more time just hanging out with them and talking and then guiding them into very deep and significant discussions about intimacy with God, sexual purity, accountability, parenting, marriage, and a million other topics vital to being a man of God. The biblical truths are the same; he just has to get there in a different way.

Another friend of mine, John, joined the college staff as layleader and is leading a Bible study for men on Monday evenings on a local college campus. Again, he's taking the principles he has learned about ministry to men and is now applying them to a bunch of college-age men, my son included.

6. *Relationship, relationship, relationship.* This group of men values relationship above everything else. For the past several years I have been working with the internship program here at Elmbrook—in fact, it is one of the favorite things I do. I love interacting with these young men and women who are working for the first time in the church and seeking to discover God's call on their lives. We normally meet every Monday afternoon, and I will often ask them what they did over the weekend. The answer is always the same: "We just hung out." Matter of fact, if I had a nickel for every time they said it, I would be a millionaire. If you want to have a ministry to Gen Y, learn to enjoy coffee, find a comfortable seat at Starbucks, and just hang out. Community and relationship is so important to them that they will need to belong before they believe. I can tell you right now that you will not be able to impact this group from a distance; it will only be through proximity to them. I said it earlier, I'll say it again: The closer you get to these men, the greater the impact you will have in their lives. Within these relationships they are looking for encouragement and empowerment to become the man that God desires them to be. They really need someone to believe in them, someone who is in their corner cheering them on.

7. *Let the storytelling begin.* It should be no surprise that a generation of people who grew up on TV and videos loves a good story. They view life as one big story and they want to know their part in that story. This of course works wonderfully to your advantage when talking to them about Christianity. The epoch story is the story of God's work in the world from creation forward. Many of us like to share the four spiritual laws and think the entire gospel can be summarized in four statements, while the story of the Bible is much grander. The applications are numerous. First, you will want to allow time in your small groups for men to share their stories with one another and help them understand where their story intersects with God's greater story. Second, when it comes to preaching and Bible study, they are very interested in the narrative texts and you can spend a great deal of time there. Again, as an older generation, we have naturally been drawn to Paul's letters and all the

theology it brings with it, but not this group. They love the Jesus story and what it teaches and what he stands for. They want the rich background to the texts for a deeper understanding. In your teaching, you will want to use stories to illustrate your points, and the more personal the better. Related to this, the use of testimony in your worship services can be very powerful if they come from the heart and talk about how God met them in the messiness of life.

There is a group of people in our society who would say this generation is a bunch of slackers, whiners, and homebodies who are going to amount to nothing. But there is another group, myself included, who would say this generation of men is going to storm the gates of hell here and around the world. I can tell you right now, you may get frustrated at times, you will be challenged by tough questions and skeptical attitudes, but you will be inspired by their faith, compassion, and willingness to take risks for Jesus. Don't be afraid of them; draw close, listen, cheer, and watch as God raises up a whole new generation for him.

Books on Ministry to Generation Y

UnChristian by David Kinnaman and Gabe Lyons

The Leadership Jump by Jimmy Long

Transformissional Coaching by Steve Ogne and Tim Roehl

Generating Hope by Jimmy Long

Mentoring Leaders by Carson Pue

Getting Real by Ken Baugh and Rich Hurst

Church Next by Eddie Gibbs

The Emerging Church by Dan Kimball

NOTES

1. Josh McDowell and Bob Hostetler, *The New Tolerance* (Carol Stream, IL: Tyndale House, 1998), 208.

Effective Small Groups

10

The book and movie *Band of Brothers* follows a World War II infantry company as the men go through training, their first jump at Normandy, and excursions all over the European theater. Drawing on hours of interviews with survivors, as well as the soldiers' journals and their letters home, Stephen Ambrose recounts the stories, often in the men's own words, of these American heroes. He tells how this band of brothers fought, went hungry, froze, and died together.

The men of Easy Company, 506th Parachute Infantry Regiment, 101st Airborne Division, U.S. Army, came from different parts of the country. They were farmers and coal miners, mountain men and sons of the Deep South. Some were desperately poor, others from the middle class. One came from Harvard, one from Yale, and a couple from UCLA. Only one was from the Old Army, only a few came from the National Guard or Reserves. They were citizen soldiers.

They came together in the summer of 1942, by which time the Europeans had been at war for three years. By the late spring of 1944, they had become an elite company of airborne light infantry. Early on the morning of D-Day, in its first combat action, Easy Company captured and put out of action a German battery of four 105mm cannons that were looking down on the Utah Beach. The company led the way into Carentan, fought in Holland, held the perimeter at Bastogne, led the counteroffensive in the Battle of the Bulge, fought in the Rhineland campaign, and took Hitler's Eagle's Nest at Berchtesgaden. It had taken almost 150 percent casualties. At the peak of its effectiveness, in Holland in October 1944 and in the Ardennes in January 1945, it was as good a rifle company as there was in the world. The job completed, the company disbanded, the men went home.[1]

From Genesis 1 forward, God has been calling his people to live in community. Every man needs his own band of brothers. He needs a place to belong, a place where he is accepted for who he is, a place where he can tell his story, a place where his wounds can be healed, a place where his dreams can be shared, his heart refreshed, and his gifts used. Men are in desperate need of a safe place where they can become all that God desires them to be. It bears repeating—a men's small group, operating properly, is the optimal place for a man to grow spiritually.

If you are a pastor or men's leader, I encourage you to do everything possible to get every man in your church into a men's small group. This chapter will address how to effectively lead a small group. (I discuss how to start small groups in my previous book, *How to Build a Life-Changing Men's Ministry.*) While there are entire books written on how to start and lead effective small groups, some of which I will mention at the end of the chapter, here we'll cover the basics of leading an effective group. I will start walking you through the life stages of a group, followed by the principles for leading a group, and will finish the chapter with some ideas on how to get started. I can tell you right now that one of the greatest joys you will ever experience in ministry to men is leading a group of men into a deeper walk with Jesus and deeper relationships with one another.

Why a Band of Brothers?

Now, there still may be a few of you who are not convinced that men need small groups. If you happen to be in that camp, let me draw upon the story of Easy Company and share a few reasons why small groups are so important, and some of the incredible things that happen when men connect with one another.

    1. *There is a battle raging all around us.* When the soldiers of Easy

Company were dropped onto the beach at Normandy, the bullets were flying and there were already heavy casualties. It is no different today. The spiritual battle is very real, the bullets are flying, and there are casualties everywhere you look. Satan has a two-prong strategy. First, to blind the eyes of unbelievers so they never see the truth of who Jesus is and what he has done for us. Second, to take out those who call upon the name of Jesus any way he can.

One of the greatest problems we have in the Western church culture is our peacetime mentality where we believe all is well in the land of prosperity! Look around, though. There are wounded guys everywhere. Some are wounded spiritually, some emotionally, others relationally, and still others vocationally. But one thing is sure: Almost every man I know is wounded in one way or another, and there is absolutely no way men can survive in this world alone. Isolation is not masculinity, it is stupidity. One of my favorite scenes in the movie *Black Hawk Down* is when a Humvee has been sent into the city to pick up the wounded soldiers and the sergeant tells one of the soldiers to get into the car and drive. When the soldier says, "I can't, I'm shot," the sergeant looks at him and responds, "We are all shot. Now get into the truck and drive." We are all shot and we all need a safe place for healing.

2. *They fought together.* When the men of Easy Company landed at Normandy and fought in the Battle of the Bulge, they did it together. No one was sent alone, because it was too dangerous. It would have been suicide. The lone-ranger approach to Christianity and serving just does not work. Gentlemen, we are involved in a battle bigger than ourselves, and a men's small group is a great place to minister together and lock arms to serve the community and the world. I just love the passage in Philippians 2:25 where Paul describes his relationship to Epaphroditus as a fellow brother, worker, and soldier: "But I think it is necessary to send back to you Epaphroditus, my brother, fellow worker and fellow soldier, who is also your messenger, whom you sent to take care of my needs."

What a description of a small group! It is about serving the poor of your city together, building a home together, working with college students, tutoring at-risk kids, or reaching out into your neighborhood together. When I first started the Top Gun Ministry nearly twenty years ago, our motto was simply, "Become friends and change the world." Men are looking for a place where they can lock arms with other like-minded men and move out into the world and make a difference for Christ.

3. *They trained together.* The soldiers came from all segments of society, most with no military training at all. They spent months learning what was needed to be the best of the best. Unfortunately, most men today have absolutely no training in what it means to be a godly man. Good men, yes, nice men, yes, but not godly men. A men's small group is a place to train men spiritually. It is the place where they can learn about the spiritual disciplines and incorporate them into their lives. It is the place where they can work on their character and address the issues that are hidden from the world. They can discover and develop the gifts God has entrusted to them. They can learn to relate to other men, forgive, handle conflict, serve, pray, and accept. In a small group men will become the man God wants them to be. It is the optimal place for growth, equipping, and training.

4. *They encouraged one another.* The men of Easy Company accepted and affirmed one another. Their nights were filled with storytelling, reading each other's letters, and encouraging one another. They needed each other. Leaders, your men need a place to be encouraged, accepted, and built up. They are beat up all week long. They need to know someone is in their corner and wants them to win at life. Encouragement is such a powerful thing in a man's life; he cannot live without it. Your men can be encouraged and cheered on when they take a step of faith, say no to sin, break through a fear, share at a deeper level, and act in obedience.

5. *They built lifelong friendships.* The men of Easy Company stayed connected until the day they died. The friendships they developed were deep; they were built on loyalty, sacrifice, honesty, and trust. This sounds like something every man needs and desires. Unfortunately, most men are relationally challenged. They don't know how to make friends. Within the context of a men's small group, they have the opportunity to develop some lifelong friends. I know I have. Other than my family, my small-group friendships are among the most precious to me. The men of your

church are looking for the same thing. They know that the quality of their life will be determined by the relationships they develop.

Qualities of an Effective Small-Group Leader

Now, let's get into the practical aspects of leading a group. An effective small-group leader . . .

Models (*1 Timothy 4:12*)—I am not talking about modeling clothes. What is important is that you be a man who models Jesus in your speech, life, love, faith, and purity. An effective leader will never ask a group member to do anything he is not willing to do himself. If you expect men to be vulnerable, you need to demonstrate vulnerability by sharing from an emotional level. Prayer is another area where men need to see a working model—someone who shows them how to pray and who leads a daily, prayer-filled life. The age-old saying is true when it comes to leading a small group: Christianity is caught more than taught. One model of a Christlike life is worth a thousand words.

Motivates (*1 Thessalonians 5:11*)—A good leader creates a winning environment. (I will share what that looks like in a few pages.) A motivator is able to work with men wherever they are in life, encouraging them and guiding them to become more like Jesus Christ. When progress is being made, a motivator will acknowledge and affirm what God is doing in their lives. Creating an environment for growth includes believing in your men, loving and accepting them, allowing them to take risks, and remaining committed to them even when they fail.

Multiplies (*2 Timothy 2:2*)—An effective small-group leader is someone who wants to advance the kingdom of God by building into the lives of men so they will do the same with others. This type of man wants to leave a legacy behind with those in whom he has invested his life. This leader is living for the next generation. Early in the process of leading they will begin to identify at least one man to be an apprentice who can start taking leadership roles in the group. They will have them open in prayer, lead a sharing time, get together with one of the group members, or lead the discussion, all in preparation for leading their own group. Every leader needs to see the development of other leaders as one of their chief goals. He is willing to take the time to build the vision for evangelism and discipleship into a small group of men who will likewise take the torch of faith across the street, around the world, and on to the next generation.

Mentors (*1 Thessalonians 2:8–9*)—A mentor believes in the principle that ministry happens best in friendship. An effective small-group leader has a strong desire to really get to know men and enjoys spending time with them. The type of person you are looking for is a man who enjoys initiating relationships with other men. He knows the value of maintaining friendships with the men in a group and can communicate commitment to his friends. A mentor must be willing to see others succeed, cheer on the men in their group, and help them with their roles, goals, and souls.

Ministers (*1 Peter 5:2–3*)—Finally, a small-group leader has the heart of a shepherd with the compassion to accept his men where they are and give care to them, just as Jesus would. The shepherd's role is to lead, teach, and protect. He will minister out of a grateful heart, knowing that in all circumstances he is privileged to pass on the comfort and direction he has received from Jesus.

Stages of a Small Group

One book that has been instrumental in our small-group training has been Geoff Gorsuch's book *Brothers*. Our new leaders read it and discuss it at our training sessions. In the book, Geoff describes the stages that every men's small group goes through over time. Allow me to give a quick overview of what Geoff says, but I recommend you read it yourself for a full description of each stage.

Stage One—Becoming Acquaintances—Romans 15:7

Principle: This initial phase of a small group is characterized by men building trust in one another. It takes time; you cannot hurry the process.[2]

Key characteristics of this phase:

- Overcoming men's fear of closeness and intimacy

- Identifying clear goals and the purpose of the group

- Avoiding too much structure

- Creating a safe environment for relating

- Agreeing on confidentiality

Key questions to answer:
- Who should be in the group?

- Will it be open or closed?

- Where and when will we meet?

- What are we going to do?

Stage Two—Building Friendships—1 Thessalonians 5:11

Principle: This phase is characterized by men gaining confidence in each other and learning to encourage one another. They will experience some conflict, which is normal, and they will learn to manage it.[3]

Key characteristics of this phase:
- Understanding, not competing

- Commitment to the process of confession and forgiveness as a means of reconciliation

- Ability to agree to disagree

- Development of discussion skills and the art of asking good questions

- Development of conflict resolution skills

- Addressing subjects relevant to men

Stage Three—Bonding as Brothers—Colossians 3:16; Ephesians 4:15

Principle: This phase is characterized by men exhorting one another to growth and service. This will include becoming interdependent and accountable to one another. Covenants are made when trust is assured.[4]

Key characteristics of this phase:

- Gives permission to those who have earned the right to respond to us in a new and honest way

- Makes covenants

- Finds real freedom and acceptance as a result of the new definition of our relationships

- Significant change takes place

- Introduces worship and accountability to the group

Stage Four—Christlikeness—John 17:23

Principle: The last phase is characterized by men finding their place of service in the body of Christ and taking on leadership roles in the group and in the world.[5]

Key characteristics of this phase:

- Finding your place and serving within the body of Christ

- Continuing the process of sanctification through serving

- Honoring the body of Christ and your local pastor

- Becoming a servant leader

Preparation of a Small-Group Leader

With this background information in mind, let's move on to how one prepares for a weekly small-group meeting. I can still remember my coaching days when our head coach would say, "To fail to prepare is to prepare to fail." This rings true when leading a weekly small-group meeting. An unprepared leader is a liability to any small group, and men quickly pick up on this. If you are not prepared, why should they be? When it comes to the actual study, it takes time and work for it to be fruitful. Don't procrastinate. If your group is going through a book, don't rely on your study notes from the last time you read it. Read it again. As you are preparing for the lesson, think and pray about the Scripture's main objective and what you want your group to learn from it. Prepare questions to move the discussion in that direction and lead to personal application points.

The final part of your preparation, but not the least important, is to spend time individually (and with your co-leader) praying for the upcoming lesson. Pray that God would have his way and visit that meeting through the work of the Holy Spirit. Also, spend time praying for each of the group members during the course of the week. One section of Scripture I use to pray for others is Colossians 1:9–12.

CReating a SafE EnvironmEnt

When it comes to actually leading a group of men, here are a few principles to keep in mind when building a healthy group.

PRincIPLE #1: TiME, TiME, TiME

You cannot speed up the process of deep relationships. I have seen men take up to a year to develop authentic and vulnerable relationships with one another. When starting your group, you will want to spend more time in relationship-building than in the actual study time. We have found that spending a long evening together is an excellent way to jump-start relationship building. During the evening you can share a meal and also allow each man to share his story. It does not need to be his testimony—only his life story, which may be less threatening. The leader will want to begin with his story to set the tone and be an example of vulnerability. After the initial meeting, the subsequent meetings will be geared in the direction of relationship building, 75 percent to 25 percent. Start with safe, easy questions, and as the weeks go on share deeper issues. In some ways it is like peeling an onion. As time goes on you will be able to even out the time spent between study/ discussion and your sharing and prayer time.

Principle #2: Be an Example of Vulnerability

Your group will only be as open as you are. Oftentimes a leader will meet with me and tell me that no one is sharing anything personal in their group and they are way too superficial. My response is, "How vulnerable are you with the group? Have you shared some of the skeletons from your past? Have you shared your wounds, failures, and fears?" Starting with your opening retreat or evening, you will want to set the tone for where the group is going. Being an example also comes into play in the area of accountability. You will want to be held accountable for things that matter, and ask the men to hold you to it!

Principle #3: Know What Men Need

Hopefully throughout this book you have picked up on these, but let me remind you what men need in a small-group setting.

- A place to belong—men need to know they belong and are known by others. In a society of isolationism, they need someone who knows them by name.

- A place to be accepted—for who he is without judgment.

- A place to be affirmed—they need to know someone is in their corner cheering for them.

- A place to be authentic—make it real. Allow them to take the masks off and be honest and truthful with one another.

Principle #4: Use Guiding Questions to Keep the Discussion Flowing

One of the goals for any study group is for the leader to facilitate, not teach. I have found these basic principles and questions to be very helpful in leading and facilitating. It also takes the pressure off the leader and puts more responsibility on the men.

Extending Questions—For example: "What can you add to this?" "Are there any examples of this that you can find in the Old Testament?"

"Where else in the Bible can you find that principle?" "Is there another Scripture verse related to it?"

Clarifying Questions—Two examples are, "What do you mean by that?" "Can you explain that more fully?"

Justifying Questions—"Why do you say that?" "What is the thinking behind that statement?" "Can you justify that for us?" "Where else is that found?"

Redirecting Questions—If someone tends to dominate the discussion, you can redirect the questions to other people in the group. "Jim, what do you think?" "How would you answer that?" "What are your thoughts on that?"

Summary Questions—"John, how would you summarize the last ten minutes of our discussion?" "What main principle is coming through to you from today's discussion?"

PRINCIPLE #5: FACILITATE HEALTHY COMMUNICATION

There are at least three models of communication within small groups—the best is Model C.

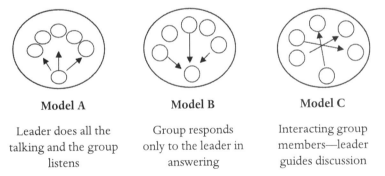

Model A	Model B	Model C
Leader does all the talking and the group listens	Group responds only to the leader in answering	Interacting group members—leader guides discussion

Model A—The leader does most of the talking and the group listens. This is obviously not effective at all in facilitating communication among group members, yet most of our teaching in the church today is based on this model.

Model B—The leader asks a question and the group responds only to the leader. This is only slightly more effective than Model A.

Model C—Interaction among group members as the leader guides the discussion. This moves the group away from black and white answers to gray areas that stimulate more interactive discussion. The goal of a good referee or umpire is to go unnoticed but keep the game going, so a good facilitator is not to dominate the group but keep it going.

Another principle for communicating effectively with one another is active listening. To actively listen means that you are participating as they talk. You are hearing them, nodding when in agreement, giving them eye contact, and discussing what you heard them say by clarifying, summarizing, and making sure you understood exactly what was said.

Although this may sound counterproductive, silence is okay. Allow for it and don't be afraid to give the group time to think, processing what they heard. After a time of silence has passed, ask, "So, what do you think about what we have been discussing?" or "How can we add to that?"

Finally, ensure your surroundings are conducive for good communication. Is your meeting place too cold or too warm? Are there distractions such as children running around or phones ringing? Is there proper lighting? Is it light enough to read and take notes but not glaring? Can everyone see each other? Are the seats comfortable?

Principle #6: Handle Prayer Time Carefully

One of the tricky aspects of leading a small group is the sharing and prayer time. You will no doubt have men in your group from a variety of backgrounds. Some have been in small groups for years and are comfortable sharing and praying out loud. Others have never been in a group, much less prayed aloud or shared about their life. Be very careful in how you handle this part of the meeting. Consider the following to encourage prayer in your group.

1. Teach by example; demonstrate how to pray.

2. Ask for prayer requests and lead by sharing what you would like them to pray for on your behalf. The leader's vulnerability in sharing his personal life can lead the group into great freedom to pray for what is REALLY on their minds.

3. Emphasize that there is no right or wrong way to pray—talk to God just as you would to anyone sitting in the group. Don't pray

because you feel pressured, but pray as you feel comfortable and desire to do so.

4. Pray short, simple prayers, not long flowery ones. Someone who has never prayed aloud will appreciate that prayer can be as simple as a sentence of praise, confession, or petition.

5. Promote the "popcorn" method of prayer, where men pray as they feel led, rather than in any particular order or sequence.

6. Encourage the ABCs of group prayer—A is for Audible, B is for Brief, and C is for Christ-centered.

7. No one has to pray aloud. They can join in when they feel comfortable.

8. Never ask a man to pray out loud unless you know he is comfortable doing so. This may mean you will need to open and close the group in prayer until you know them better.

The First Meeting

First impressions matter, especially when it comes to men's small groups. You normally get one shot with a man, and that is why we put our very best and veteran leaders in charge of new groups. We have discovered it is often the little things that set the tone of meetings. Planning, being organized, and being prepared gives group members a sense of confidence. In order to make the first meeting as smooth as possible, let me mention a few things that may help.

- Call everyone the day before the first meeting to remind them and welcome them.

- Pray for each man.

- Arrange a comfortable meeting room free of distractions.

- Use name tags—at least for a few weeks.

- Dictate a start and finish time—very important.

- Take time to explain and discuss the format for the group—how long you will meet, whether the group is open or closed to new members, what you will study, the expectations, etc.

As mentioned earlier, spend some time getting to know one another. Come up with a fun exercise to get the men to share a little about their lives. Make sure you start safe and move the men along as they are able. I am a strong believer in voluntary vulnerability and voluntary accountability. Neither can be forced. Men need only be open with their lives as they are able. As trust is built, they will share more and more. If trust is broken, they will shut down and most likely leave.

When it comes to the timing of the groups, most of our men's small groups are basically divided into the following segments:

Fellowship and opening prayer—10 minutes
Studying the lesson—45 minutes
Personal sharing and prayer—35 minutes

Starting a Group

Now you may be wondering how to actually start a men's small group. There are definitely some specific things you can do to get a group started. Start by asking God to lead you to the men he wants in the group.

Next, start making a list of men you know who may be interested in a small group. It can include guys from church, your neighborhood, workplace, or wherever. Like an insurance agent, make that list as long as you can. Once you have the list, pray over it and ask God to lead you to the men he wants in the group. As you begin to run into these men, invite them to the group. Explain what you are doing so they have a good idea of what you are asking them. If you are going to use a book, show it to them or give them a copy. Tell them when you plan to start and when you need a decision from them. They could even join a week or two into the study. I would suggest you start with a six- to eight-week commitment. It has to be short enough not to overwhelm those who have never been in a group but long enough to get some momentum going.

I would also recommend that when you're putting your list together, start with men you get along with, where there is shared interest. You don't have to start with those you don't get along with! Most of our small groups are five to eight men. If there are fewer men than that, the group can get pretty small if someone is sick or on vacation. If you have more than eight, it is easy for men not to participate and become only spectators.

Another thing you can do once you have your list is send each man an invitational letter, spelling out what you are asking of them and what you'll be doing. I do this regularly when leading my leadership small groups and find it very effective. Once the invitations have gone out, it is time to pray again for God to bring just the right men into the group. More than once I have been surprised by the men who have responded and how God directs someone who has been looking for a group to cross my path. Once the men reply, you are ready to start.

What to Do in the Group

The next step is figuring out what you should study in your group. It depends on what type of group you are starting. If it is an entry-level group, you may want to think about using something like *Man in the Mirror* by Pat Morley. We have used that book for years to start new groups because Pat touches on topics relevant to men. The chapters are not long and it makes for great discussion. Another book for entry-level groups is *The Purpose-Driven Life* by Rick Warren. It explains the basics of Christianity in a very understandable way, with plenty of Scripture references. A new booklet we have written and are using all over our community is *IronMan*. It's a nine-week study written specifically for men who have never been involved in a small group, and it slowly eases them into it.

Our entry-level groups start with a six- to eight-week commitment, and toward the end we ask the men how they enjoyed the group and if they would like to continue for another ten to twelve weeks. After tracking this for over fifteen years now, we have found that 85 percent of the men are willing to go to the next level. For our leaders, the stated goal of these entry-level groups is twofold. First, they are introduced to small groups. We want to give them the very best small-group experience we can because we know if they have a good experience, they will stick around. Second, it is an introduction to Jesus. We desire to introduce every man to Jesus during those first couple of months, and we have had many men come to Christ.

Once the group has moved from an entry-level group to a normal men's Bible study, our focus changes a bit. We have found our best groups alternate between studying a book of the Bible and using another study guide or book. When it comes to studying the Bible, our groups usually go back and forth between the Old and New Testaments. You may choose to study one chapter a week and/or use a study guide like the Life Changers series by Navigators. We encourage reading the chapter of Scripture once a day for the entire week to really allow God's Word to soak in and prepare us for discussion. The leader may read a commentary as well to get some extra background information. One nice thing this format provides is the opportunity to rotate leadership, resulting in training new leaders all the time. For a list of recommended readings, see Appendix A. This list has been compiled through the recommendations of our small-group leaders over the years.

Small-Group Killers

As a small-group leader you need to know there are certain things that can creep into a group that slowly kill it. Let me share what we have seen over the years.

Lack of mission. The first killer I see on a regular basis is a group that becomes too inwardly focused. They spend a great deal of time sharing their lives but never get off their blessed assurance and do anything. For a group to survive, they need a purpose greater than themselves. They need to be serving individually or as a group on a regular basis.

Lack of balance. Read Acts 2:42–47 and you soon discover that the early church was committed to a wide range of activities. It says the members were devoted to:

- Prayer and worship
- The Word of God
- Caring for and serving others
- Living life together

When a group focuses on one or two of these, at the exclusion of the others, it is setting itself up for failure.

Lack of group covenant. One of the first things we recommend doing with your small group is signing a group covenant. I present an example in *How to Build a Life-Changing Men's Ministry.* In brief, though, a good covenant addresses things like confidentiality, accountability, and expectations for accepting and praying for each other. Men want to know what they are committing themselves to, and the covenant does just that. I encourage groups to refer to it at least every six months to make sure they are on the same page and in agreement with what they are doing and where they are headed.

Breaking of confidentiality. One of the greatest fears a man has is sharing something with others and having it leak to those outside the group. When this happens, you are sure to lose the man and may never get him back. This breach of confidentiality is by far one of the greatest group killers. For fifteen years I spoke at the Milwaukee Brewers chapel service on Sunday mornings before the game. In the Brewer locker room there was a sign above the door that read, "What you hear here, see here, stays here." In your first session tell the guys to imagine a sign above the door that says the same thing. We tell the men they are not allowed to share things they've heard even with their wives. If a man hears about something he shared with the group in confidence, a few days or weeks later, his trust is gone and he will have a hard time sharing again. I would encourage you to build confidentiality into your group covenant.

Men who need counseling. Oftentimes someone in your group will have some deep needs or wounds that have not been dealt with, and as a result he will use the group as a support group and not a Bible study. Now, I am not saying you should not allow men who have problems to be in your small group. We all have problems. But each man has to realize there are others in the group to consider and when it comes to the sharing time, they cannot monopolize it or make it a group counseling session. When this happens, gently suggest a support group or a Christian counselor to get him the help he really needs. Then the group can serve as a support to him but not be responsible for fixing him.

Men do not feel valued. I remember Pat Morley saying that what keeps a man coming back to a small group is a leader who lets him know how much he is valued. The old saying is true, "Men do not care how much you know, until they know how much you care." If men feel they are just a number or that you are not interested in them, they will not come back.

In the summer of 1942, the men of Easy Company came together for the first time. None of the men knew each other and they had no idea what they were getting themselves into. A few years later this group of men had become a Band of Brothers, whose lives intersected at every level, whose impact was felt all over the world. It is no different for the small group you are about to start or are presently leading. The men are going to come from all over the place and are really not sure what they are getting themselves into. But I can tell you this from watching hundreds of such groups—the lives of men are going to intersect at every level. They will be transformed into the likeness of Christ, and the impact they can make will shake the gates of hell!

Recommended Reading

The Accountable Man by Tom Eisenman

Leading From Your Strengths by John Trent

Brothers by Geoff Gorsuch

The Seven Deadly Sins of Small Group Ministry by Bill Donahue and Russ Robinson

Leading Life-Changing Small Groups by Bill Donahue

NOTES

1. Stephen Ambrose, *Band of Brothers* (New York: Simon & Schuster Paperbacks, 1992), 15.

2. Geoff Gorsuch, *Brothers: Calling Men Into Vital Relationships*, (Colorado Springs: NavPress, 1994), 22.

3. Ibid., 34.

4. Ibid., 46.

5. Ibid., 60.

11

A long-time friend of mine, Mark, was diagnosed with stomach cancer in his mid-thirties. He had two young children, a beautiful wife, and a bright future ahead of him. Within the year, I was performing Mark's memorial service with over fifteen hundred people in attendance. But between diagnosis and memorial service, a great deal of significant ministry took place, and as I look back on that year, it may have been some of the most important ministry I've had. There were long walks together talking about family, life, and death. There were times of reading Scripture and praying together. After a long-shot surgery in New York, there was a quick trip to be by his bedside during the recovery stage. And there were those final precious minutes this side of heaven when we prayed, cried, sang, and said good-bye as a family. Looking back on it now, this was ministry at its best.

I have seen more pain, hurt, sickness, and death than I ever dreamed possible. Yet in the midst of it there is a sense of privilege that God allows each of us to be his ambassadors of comfort, counsel, and courage. If you are going to be involved in ministry to men, you had better be ready for men who are experiencing the loss of a loved one, the hurt of being downsized, the struggle of an addiction, the agony of making an ethical decision at work, or the pain of going through a divorce, along with a host of other difficult life-changing experiences. This chapter will provide some general guidelines for ministering to men in crisis, and we'll look at eight common situations that come up when working with men.

Start by Showing Up

The ministry of presence is vital in difficult situations. Just being with a man in crisis makes a big difference. When Jim was going through a divorce, his small-group leader went to the courthouse and sat in the audience to show his support. When Bob's child was in an accident and was rushed to the ER, a good friend showed up and sat in the waiting room, just to be there for him. When Bill lost his job, his accountability partner stopped over that night to watch the game with him. In each case, there may not have been a whole lot spoken, but there didn't have to be. It was each of those men being the presence of Jesus to their brother in pain.

One of the biggest excuses I hear for not helping men in trouble is that a person says they don't know what to say. My response is, "You don't have to say anything, just show up." We make it much more complicated than it really is. We don't need a theological degree or to be eloquent in speaking or to be a professional counselor to just show up. What you do have to have is the courage to walk into a difficult and usually painful situation in the name of Jesus. When I do this I usually just give the man a hug and tell him how sorry I am for what he is going through.

The second principle is dependence on the ministry of the Holy Spirit. In John 14, Jesus speaks extensively about the Holy Spirit's role in the life of a believer. He will be your Counselor (v. 16) and Spirit of truth (v. 17), he lives in you (v. 17), he will teach you all things (v. 26), he will remind you of everything Jesus taught (v. 26), and he will give you peace (v. 27). Now, that is quite the resource at our disposal as a minister of Jesus.

Keep in mind that God is not calling us to minister to others in our power, but rather in the power of the Holy Spirit. I can't tell you how many times I felt inadequate in a counseling situation, at the bed of someone dying, or sitting with a man whose wife just died. But our God is more than adequate, all powerful, all knowing, faithful, and with me at all times. To be involved with men will mean we will be spiritually fatigued in order to move people toward full devotion in Christ. But the key is this: He will give us the supernatural strength and explosive energy we need as we labor to move people on to maturity. Keep in mind that all we can muster cannot equal what God can do through us. You have a power source that is inexhaustible. You have seen the ads for the Energizer Bunny; it keeps going and going and going. The same is true of God's energy.

Men, it is not your energy or internal reservoirs that count. It's God's presence, his authority, his wisdom, and his power that will overcome your weariness, fears, inadequacies, depression, tiredness, and ambivalence. In 2 Corinthians 12:10 we are reminded that God loves weak people. He is not impressed with strong people or people who seem to have it all together or are self-sufficient. He is drawn to people who are weak and admit it. God loves to use ordinary, imperfect people to do extraordinary things.

Gideon's weakness was low self-esteem and deep insecurities, and God transformed him into a mighty man of valor. Abraham's weakness was fear—twice he claimed his wife was his sister to protect himself—but God transformed Abraham into the father of those who have faith. Impulsive, weak-willed Peter became a rock. The adulterer David became a man after God's own heart. John, one of the sons of thunder, became the apostle of love. It was Hudson Taylor who said, "All of God's great people were weak people." In your tiredness and weakness, the Holy Spirit can work.

The third principle is using the truth from God's Word. I know I have mentioned this before, but you will very quickly discover that the Word of God is the best tool you have in your ministry tool belt. In 2 Timothy 3:16–17, Paul says, "All Scripture is God-breathed and is useful for teaching, rebuking, correcting and training in righteousness, so that the man of God may be thoroughly equipped for every good work."

When we teach the Word of God, we are sharing what God says and reminding the men of what is right and true. It serves as a compass to get our bearings straight in a world spinning out of control. In light of his Word, we can recalibrate our hearts and minds to God's perspective on the world.

When we use the Word to rebuke, we point out when something is not in accordance with God's desires. There may be times when you will need to come alongside a man and talk to him about an area of his life that is not in line with God's will. When a man is involved in an addiction or having an affair, you will need to use Scripture to bring truth to the situation. When Paul uses the word *correcting,* he is referring to the Word of God being useful for helping a man get back on track. When a man has had a moral failure, the Scriptures speak of God's forgiveness, making things right, and providing a framework for what relationships are to look like. In ministry to men you will have many correcting times.

And finally, Paul says the Word is useful for training in righteousness. This means to make us more like Jesus. Isn't this the goal—for all men to be more like Jesus? The Scriptures will help us teach our men what it means to love God and to love others. Scripture takes you into the very heart of God; it is his love letters to us. No matter what you do to earn a living, there are always "tools of the trade." If you sell cars, it's the Blue Book. If you are a plumber, it's a wrench. If you are a teacher, it's a blackboard. If you're a cook, it's pots and pans. If you are ministering to men, it's the Bible. No matter what situation you find yourself in, you will use the Word of God.

A fourth overarching principle is prayer. Prayer unleashes God's power, peace, and presence into the most difficult of situations. When driving to a hospital to visit someone, I pray for a fulfilling conversation. Before I meet someone for counseling, I pray for wisdom and guidance. When a man calls me after receiving devastating news, I pray with him on the phone. When ending a conversation with someone in the halls, I will often ask if I can pray for them—and we pray right there.

We end our men's breakfasts by telling the men to come up front if they would like to pray with someone. Man after man will approach me, share their story, and we pray together. Just this week I was with a good friend who was leaving his home for the final time to move into a hospice. To say the least, it was traumatic. His family gathered together and we prayed for him and them: that they would know God's comfort, strength, and presence in this very difficult time. Men, there is no greater ministry than the ministry of prayer, putting the lives and situations of men into the hands of our loving, gracious Father and asking for his will to be done.

A fifth principle is the ministry of listening. As men, we have an insatiable desire to fix everything, including the men and situations we work with. Unfortunately, in crisis situations there is no easy solution, and the best thing you can do is listen with the intent of hearing, not fixing. Yesterday I met with a man who was going to court for his divorce hearing. After starting our time together in prayer, I asked him how things were going and how he felt about the hearing. For the next half hour he poured out his heart to me. I didn't say a word, and didn't need to. He just needed to talk and be heard. Last week a man came in with severe problems with his son, and after asking him how things were at home, he cried out in pain for forty minutes about his son. Again, I did not say a word. I just kept eye contact with him and actively listened. When we were through he said, "Steve, I can't tell you how helpful this has been." I thought to myself, *What did I do?* I barely said a thing. I just listened. For many men and in many situations, listening is just what they need.

There are a couple of things I have found helpful in this area.

Time is on your side—You do not have to rush to a solution or an answer. Just give the man plenty of time to share his story or situation with you.

Ask questions to draw a man out—Develop the skill of asking question to get to the heart of the situation. Asking how he feels helps a man process what is going on inside of him. You are seeking to understand him and the situation.

Know your limits—As helpers, we all have limits to what we can do, and we need to know our limits. There are professionals who can help where we can't. For example, if a man comes to me with an addiction, I know I cannot help him break that addiction. I need to refer him to a counselor who deals with addiction. I can support him while he goes through treatment, but I will not be the one providing the treatment; it is beyond me. In so many of these cases you will discover that your main role is walking with them as others provide the main care or counseling.

Point to the appropriate resource—Once you know your limits, it is important to know what resources are available in your community that you can point men toward. Layleaders can refer men to their pastor. But you will also want to know who the Christian counselors are in your area. Are there Alcoholics Anonymous and sexual-addiction groups in your community? Is someone running a group for those who are unemployed?

The final principle is the ministry of serving or compassion. In Mark 10:42–45, Jesus speaks very clearly and powerfully to the disciples about servantship as the identity of a Christian. Society talks about leadership with terms like power, leverage, influence, vision, making things happen, control, credentials, experiences, and degrees. Jesus turns it on its head and speaks of compassion, humility, gentleness, generosity, patience, the good of others, and the building of his body of believers. You and I, as followers of Christ, are servants of God. As men committed to ministering to other men, our primary call is to serve them in life. You cannot separate your call to follow Christ and serve Christ. When you get involved with men, you will find yourself in a whole host of difficult and dirty situations, and oftentimes you will have no idea what to do. It is then you discover the one thing you can do is serve them, even in the smallest way. Let me share with you three reminders when it comes to serving your men.

First, servants make themselves available to serve. Servants of God do not fill up their schedules with pursuits that could limit their availability. They want to be ready to jump in when called. Some of us have so much going on that we simply do not have time for people with problems. In 2 Timothy 2:4, Paul says, "No one serving as a soldier gets involved in civilian affairs—he wants to please his commanding officer." Real servants do not only serve when convenient; they wake up saying, "God, I am available today to serve you." Interruptions won't frustrate you as much because your agenda will be whatever God wants to bring into your life. Interruptions are God's divine appointments for ministry. The servant's prayer is, "God, I am available today to be used by you in any way you wish." Let me tell you, that is a dangerous prayer!

Second, servants pay attention to the needs of others. Servants are always looking to help others. Often we are so set on accomplishing our to-do list that we miss what God is doing. Listen for signs of pain and hurt when talking with others. One question I often ask when counseling is, "How can I best minister to you in this situation?" Why leave it up to guesswork? Just ask them. Every situation is different and we need to be observant to how we can best serve them. I can still remember a few years ago when I was teaching my boys to play golf. We were at the driving range using my clubs. I started by teaching them how to hold the club, what the correct stance is, and how to swing. Tim was hitting the balls out there very nicely, but Jon was really struggling. I had him try a few different things and nothing seemed to work. Finally, in frustration he looked at me and said, "Dad, you know I am left-handed!" No wonder! I had looked right past the obvious, and that is what we do in so many situations. The servant's prayer has opened my eyes to see the needs of others.

Third, servants are faithful with what God has entrusted to them. Do not worry about the size of your task. The size is irrelevant. What you are responsible for is being faithful to what and who God has entrusted to you. We may think it is not big enough or important enough. Servants finish their tasks, fulfill their responsibilities, keep their promises, and complete their commitments. Jesus specialized in doing menial tasks: washing feet, helping children, fixing breakfast, and serving lepers. Nothing was beneath him, because he came to serve. Small tasks show a big heart. Your servant's heart is seen in little acts that others do not think of doing. Great opportunities often disguise themselves in small tasks. The race to be a leader is crowded, but the field is wide open for those willing to be a servant. The servant's prayer helps me to be faithful with what you have given me.

One of the greatest gifts my father gave us kids was his servant spirit. He served behind the scenes in the church I grew up in for as long as I can remember. He visited the hospitalized, taught Sunday school, served on boards, helped with the youth program, and cleaned the church property. My father would do whatever needed to be done. There was never any time that was inconvenient or a cost he was not willing to pay, all for the kingdom of God. My father modeled servanthood. He was always available and faithful with what God gave him, and he did not seek the applause of crowds. This example has served me well in ministering to men.

Before I get to some practical helps for times of crisis, let me just say this: Of all the vision casting, training, and teaching I have done, without a doubt the greatest joy has come from walking with men who are in pain, near the end of life, struggling for their marriage, fighting for their children, or dealing with the loss of their job. It is in those moments, the crises of life, that God calls us to step in and be his representative, his ambassador of love, grace, and truth. Our call is to simply walk with men through life, sharing our struggles and joys along the way. To laugh and cry, listen and share, model and learn, serve and be served, love and be loved.

In one of my favorite movies, *The Lord of the Rings: Return of the King*, there is a scene where Sam and Frodo are climbing the mountain to destroy the ring. Frodo is exhausted and Sam says to him, "I cannot carry your burden, but I can carry you." He proceeds to pick him up and carry him up the mountain, thus helping him to fulfill the mission he had for his life. What is ministry to men? It is walking with them and at times putting an arm around them and carrying them so they can fulfill the mission God has for them.

CRISIS POINTS
LOSS OF A JOB

For a man, this is one of the most traumatic things he will ever go through because his identity is so strongly tied to what he does. In some ways it is like a death for him, and it's a serious emotional blow. My friend Gary Hansen has a ministry called Inspired Calling (www.inspiredcalling. com), which does training for churches and works with individuals who have lost their jobs. He has four principles that are very helpful when ministering to men who have recently lost their jobs.[1]

Rebuild emotional stability. Most people are caught off guard when informed of the loss of their employment. The emotions involved in processing this trauma are real and intense. It would be very helpful for you to help them process their emotions and help pull them out of the whirlpool of doubt and fear.

Encourage spiritual growth. Many men buy into Satan's lie that God is punishing them by taking away their employment. Much of their early anger and blame is directed toward God. We can help them understand that God has them right where he wants them, and they can use this extra time as an opportunity to get close to the Lord and grow in their faith like never before. We can be the conduit of hope and future for them.

Build relational bonds. One of the most common reactions of men who have lost their job is to withdraw and isolate themselves from family and friends. In their isolation they can play the victim card, have a pity party, and simply quit. It is now more than ever when they need a group of men around them to pray for them, encourage them, and walk with them.

Improve job-search skills. Skills are learned and relearned. Unfortunately, many men are still using the same job-search techniques they learned when they left school. Many don't realize the process of searching for a job has been changed forever due to the Internet. If your church does not have a ministry like this, you may want to find one in the community to use as a referral.

Find a place to serve. Men like action and want to be accomplishing something. One of the things we have found very helpful is to put them to work in the church. We have given them certain projects that oftentimes are in line with their gifts and passions. They have done much kingdom building during their time off, and this has given them a sense of significance in the midst of the job search.

Loss of a Loved One

I have done way too many memorial services in my years, and this is by far some of the most difficult ministry there is. When burying a child, a wife, or a parent of one of your men, emotions are raw. They are looking for comfort and a word of hope and truth from God. While it's the most difficult ministry, it is one of the most meaningful ministries you will ever have. Here are a few things to keep in mind:

Presence, presence, presence. Nowhere is this more important. When you receive news that a friend, small-group member, neighbor, or work associate has lost a loved one, do all you can just to be there for him. You don't have to say much, but your presence says I love you, I am sorry, and I am here for you. If you are not that close to the person, even attending the funeral can be especially meaningful. A good friend of mine had a work associate whose mother died, so he drove two hours to the funeral. When he walked in, the woman just started to cry. She could not believe that Mike drove all that way for a funeral. It is just another chance to be the hands and feet of Jesus.

Provide practical needs. At the time of a death, the family's schedule is thrown completely out of whack, and there is a great need for outside help. It could be bringing them food, offering your home for out-of-town guests, giving them gift cards to go out to dinner, or cleaning the house after everyone has left. The best policy is just to ask how you can help them during this time—or be proactive and offer one of the ideas mentioned above and follow through in a timely fashion. It's also nice to send the person a card on the anniversary of his loved one's death, just so he knows someone is thinking of him.

Talk about grief. One myth is that people will be able to walk through the grief in one year. But to work through all the stages of grief can take much longer, and they need to know there will always be a hole in their life. It can take two years or more for people to grieve the loss of a loved one—but everyone grieves differently. Some will isolate themselves, others joke around, others journal, and others talk it through. I encourage families to be very gracious during this time. I remind families that it hits people at different times and in different ways. It is like ocean waves coming at you. You can be walking down the road a year later and think of something, and you just start crying without knowing why—it is grief.

a Man Facing Death

Over the years I have had the privilege to walk with a number of men and close friends who have died. There is something special about spending time with men who love Jesus and fully understand that this is their temporary residence and heaven is their permanent home. These men have a real sense of the eternal. They have let go of the things of this world and are looking forward to being with Jesus. Here are a few things I have learned from these men.

Read Scripture and pray. These men have told me that the reading of Scripture has been one of the most helpful things I could do for them. I simply asked them what they wanted to hear. If they do not have something specific, I read passages that speak of God's love, sovereignty, presence, and the promises of heaven (Romans 8; Psalm 139; Psalm 91; Psalm 103; Psalm 23; 2 Corinthians 4–5; John 14). We also pray for them and their surviving family members.

Talk about going home. These men needed someone to talk to about eternal things. Many people are afraid to address the subject, but I have found it very freeing to address the subject head on. When they have accepted they are going to die, I ask them how they feel about it and what their fears are. During these times it is important to remind them of what is true. You cannot remind them of the promises of Scripture often enough. I will take them to John 14:1–6 and discuss what it means for Jesus to be coming back to take them home. One thing on their minds is if they left a legacy or whether their life mattered. You cannot tell them enough that they lived a good life, they are finishing strong, and God would be proud of them.

Help them take care of final matters. One of the things I have helped a number of men do is either make a video for their children or wife to watch at an appropriate time, or write letters to be read later. There have also been times we have met with the funeral home to plan their memorial service. Recently I was asked to mediate a meeting of reconciliation. What a beautiful thing to see two family members coming together before one of them died.

Visit them. It is helpful to call ahead and see how they are doing that day. There are some days they just want to sleep and are in no condition to see someone. When they are up to it, spend some time with them, whether it is taking a walk with them, sitting by their bed, reading to them, or praying for them. Don't stay too long; if in doubt, leave early.

Pornography

Almost weekly I meet with a man who is crying because his wife discovered his use of pornography, or he lost his job because of it. It is no surprise; the statistics tell us that over 60 percent of men in the church struggle with it. Once in a while a man who has been convicted of his sin wants to know what to do about it, and he'll call me. In all cases, there are certain things that need to be done to help set him free.

Give them hope. They are wondering, *Can I be forgiven? Will my wife forgive me? Will I ever be set free?* These men need to hear the truth of God regarding his forgiveness (Colossians 2; 1 John 1; Psalm 103), and his power in their lives (1 John 4:4; John 11; Philippians 4). I take them right to Scripture and get God's Word on the subject rather than mine. They need to know that God is in the business of changing lives; it is what he does best. No one is beyond the grace and love of God.

Get them connected. Normally these men will isolate themselves because of the guilt and shame, but what they need is other men who will accept them, love them, and hold them accountable. The accountability has to occur regularly throughout the week. If a man is in sales and on the road, then the group can take turns calling him at night to check in. We have a support group for men who are dealing with sexual sins, and the group leader is excellent at walking with these men. If you don't have a support group, then connect him with a men's group that is willing to address the issue head on.

Establish guardrails. Proverbs 4:23 it says, "Guard your heart, for it is the wellspring of life." These guardrails have to do with what they watch, where they go, and who they are with. It will mean getting a filter on the computer, getting rid of certain cable stations, stopping some subscriptions, and saying there are some places he just cannot go.

Deal with the real issue. Any counselor will tell you that these issues are not about sex but something much deeper. It could be deep-rooted shame, a wound from the past, or some other unresolved emotional issue. Too often we try a little behavior modification and think things will be fine, but they aren't. Until the real underlying issues are identified and dealt with, the problem will continue. That is why I recommended

Steve Gallagher's book *At the Altar of Idolatry*, because it deals with the heart issues.

Talk to their wife. To tell or not to tell? This can be controversial, but I always recommend a man tell his wife of his struggle. If he doesn't, there will be a secret between them, and this can be divisive in the relationship. Once over the shock and anger, she can become a real support and help in dealing with the issue. It will mean going through a tunnel of chaos, but in the end it can strengthen their marriage.

Moral Failure

Every one of us is sinful and has to regularly confess our sins to God and seek his forgiveness and cleansing. However, there are times when a man will be involved in a more serious type of sin that has dire consequences, such as an affair or a crime. In each of these cases it is important to deal properly with everyone involved. For our purposes here, I will address men who have had affairs, but the principles apply to other failures as well.

Regain relational equilibrium. The first concern is their marriage and what effect this will have on it. It will be important to meet with them as a couple to begin the process of reconciliation. There will be a great deal of anger, sadness, and grief in the wife, and she will need time to work through the spectrum of emotions. I have found it helpful for her to be surrounded by women friends who can support her and be sounding boards. She will also need people who can speak truth to her, pray, and walk with her.

Regain trust. Her emotional bank account has been completely depleted, and it will take months, if not years, to be replenished. He needs to understand that she has absolutely no reason in the world to trust him and she will question everything he does, every place he goes, and every person he talks with. In the same way one has to regain the trust of the bank after bankruptcy, so the man has to show himself faithful in the little things to slowly regain her trust.

Cut off the relationship. The relationship with the other woman must be completely broken off. They can no longer be friends, call, text, or e-mail. I have had a couple of guys who have switched jobs because they could no longer work with the person.

Experience God's forgiveness. There is no sin that cannot be forgiven. It may take a while to believe and comprehend, but it is true. You may want to prepare some 3″ x 5″ cards with a number of verses that speak to God's forgiveness that he can keep with him and pull out on a regular basis. He needs to know that just because he has been forgiven does not mean there are not consequences to his sin, and the consequences may be drastic.

Help him learn from his failure. Failure that is not learned from is wasted pain. God can use our failure to teach us lessons and prepare us for the future. Once some time has passed after the fall, talk to him about what steps got him to that point and what guardrails need to be put in place to make sure it does not happen again. This process of self-understanding is vital to growth toward Jesus.

Midlife Crisis

Each of us has heard our share of midlife crisis jokes, yet the longer I work with men, the more I realize it to be a reality. It can take the form of everything from buying a Corvette to much more serious things like being apathetic about their faith, having an affair, or relapsing into a former drug or alcohol habit. It just amazes me what men will get into and how they can completely forget the principles they have lived with most of their lives. Here are a few thoughts for you to consider when working with these guys.

Identify sources of the self-destruction. The reasons could be numerous, and through conversation you can help the man look back and work through what unresolved issue has contributed to the behavior. For example, it could be that he's declining physically or has a sense of dissatisfaction after getting to the top of the ladder and realizing it is not all it is cracked up to be. It may stem from not being satisfied with his marriage, or he may have more play money than ever before. There could be many reasons for it, but help him identify why.

Help develop a sense of significance. Men in their late forties and fifties need to be involved in something bigger than themselves; something that has eternal ramifications and will give them a sense of significance.

So whether it is serving on the board of a city ministry, tutoring high school students, getting involved in an overseas ministry, or leading a new initiative in the church, these men need to know that all is not wasted and they can still make a difference.

Confrontation. I have rarely seen these men snap out of it by themselves; it usually takes a couple of men confronting him about his behavior. I usually ask others who know him well and are respected by him to do the confronting. It needs to be done according to the principles found in Scripture. He needs to know the men love him and want the best for him. With a confrontation, you will want to stick to the facts of his behavior and stay away from what you personally think.

Help him come back to the Lord. Usually in these cases the man has slowly drifted from his relationship with the Lord and needs to come back to him just as the prodigal son eventually came home. He will need help reestablishing the spiritual disciplines in his life and relearning obedience to Christ, and he'll need to see what it means to surrender every area of his life to the lordship of Jesus.

Marriage Problems

Other than men struggling with pornography, this is probably the issue I deal with the most. Unfortunately, by the time they come to you, a great deal of damage has already been done. The situations I see so often are couples who have been married for twenty-plus years getting divorced. The children were the center of the marriage and the couple poured all their time and energy into the kids, so when the kids left they had no relationship. I find that most of my work with couples is triage, usually needing to connect them with a counselor as soon as possible. Here are a few things I keep in mind:

It is going to take time and work. They need to know that in the same way their marriage did not just fall apart, so it will not just heal by itself with time. They are going to have to work at it very hard if they want it to survive. I find it important to put together a plan of action for them individually and together. This can involve reading books, going on dates, and working on relational exercises together. The plan is very specific and intentional.

Meet with both of them. If I meet with the man or the wife, I will usually only hear half the story. I'll get both sides of the story if I meet with both of them. I normally ask a lot of questions and really seek to understand where each of them is coming from, where they have been hurt, and what key issues need to be addressed. And I will ask each of them if they are interested in saving the marriage and are willing to put the time and energy into it.

Refer to a Christian counselor or mentor couple. In most cases there is some pretty severe damage already done, and one or two sessions with a pastor is not going to fix it. I recommend they meet with a professional. If they are unable to do that or if the situation has not gotten to that point, I try to find an older couple they could meet with on a regular basis to walk with them for a while and talk through the issues they are facing.

Establish a prevention defense. When my wife and I speak at marriage conferences we will always tell couples the same thing: talk daily, date weekly, and retreat yearly. This has served us very well over the past twenty-six years of marriage. To have a healthy strong marriage does not just happen; it takes work. For us, we take at least fifteen to twenty minutes each day to talk about what is going on in our lives. We have been out on a date almost every week of our marriage to build the relationship, and we take three to five days each year to get away and build our marriage. We are constantly reading books on marriage and discussing them. One final thing: If you know of a couple who is getting married, highly suggest they go through extensive premarital counseling and classes. All the studies have shown that the more that is done ahead of time, the better.

Uncontrolled Anger

Men funnel 90 percent of their emotions through anger. So if they are sad about a parent dying, they are probably not able to say so; they will just kick the cat. If they are apprehensive about a sales presentation the next day, they kick the cat. Most men have stuffed their emotions so deep they have no clue what is going on inside of them emotionally, and as a result it comes out in very inappropriate ways, like kicking the cat! With that in mind, here are some things I have been trying to do with our men.

Seek to understand. Help a man step back and seek to understand what is really going on when he starts to feel anger. He needs to ask himself why he is angry. Has he been hurt in some way? Is he fearful about something, or frustrated, or has there been an injustice? We need to help our men begin to identify what is really going on emotionally and then express it in a healthy manner. In order to help him, you might have to suggest some emotional words for him to choose from, or you may want to ask him questions that force him to process what is going on inside emotionally. For example, I may ask him to talk about how he feels about losing his job. Or if there's a death, what he misses most about the person and how it makes him feel. These types of questions help him process his real emotions.

Learn to express emotions in a healthy manner. Instead of pushing it down or acting like there is nothing wrong, we can help men express their anger or other emotions in a healthy manner. They can learn to call it what it is and go to the person they are angry with, then confess it to that person in a manner that is appropriate. This involves telling the person why they are angry and seeking to reconcile with the person. If they come to the realization that they are not really angry but feeling something else, we can help them express that as well.

They can change. It is important for them to desire a real change, and encourage the possibility of that with the help of God. Too many men say, "It's just the way I am" or "I was born this way" or "I can't control it." This is wrong and we need to call men on it. I will ask early on whether they want to change or not. One thing that is helpful is to do an inventory of all the damage their anger has caused in their relationships, marriage, and family. Remind them that God can change them and that there is no sin too great for God.

NOTES

1. The first four principles come from a paper entitled "Inspired Calling's Career Coaching Philosophy" by Gary Hansen, and were used with permission. For more information on Inspired Calling go to www.inspiredcalling.com.

Conclusion

During my senior year of high school, our basketball team was playing at Cedarburg, which had one of the older gyms in the area. It was dimly lit and had dead spots on the wooden floor that only the home team knew about. To many it was a pit, but I enjoyed playing there. It felt something like *Hoosiers*! We were fairly evenly matched and the game went right down to the wire. But before going any further with this story, let me tell you a little about my position on the team. First, I was a good defensive player, so it was my job to take the opposing team's best offensive player and try to shut him down. Second, I always threw the ball in after the other team scored. And third, on offense my job was to set picks for my best friend and the best player on the team, Dave.

Okay, now back to the game. The second half ended in a tie, so we went into overtime, which also ended in a tie. The second overtime continued to be knotted up until eight seconds left, when Cedarburg took the lead. We brought the ball down quickly and called a time-out. With two seconds left on the clock, we huddled and the coach drew up the play. Everyone in the stands knew exactly what was going to happen. I was going to throw the ball to Dave and he would hit a shot to send it into triple overtime. The ref gave me the ball right under our basket and the players started to move. Just as we planned, Dave came around a pick and I hit him with a beautiful pass, I must say. He caught it and went up for the shot. Since everyone knew exactly what was going to happen, they double-teamed him, so instead of shooting, he passed the ball back to me. When I received the ball, I was not sure what to do with it, since I rarely touched it in bounds! I went up for the shot under the basket as time expired and missed. But under the sound of the buzzer I heard the ref's whistle; I had been fouled. With no time left on the clock, I went to the line for two free throws. If I made them, we would go into a third overtime. No one was on the line and just as the ref gave me the ball, the entire Cedarburg student section stood and started yelling things at me that I can't print here. They threw pennies at me and pointed at me and started to yell in unison, "You, you, you, you!" I wiped my hands on my socks, as I had learned at Al McGuire's basketball camp years before, and calmly hit the first free throw. The students went quiet. The ref handed me the ball for the second shot and the students started up again. The words more vulgar than before, the pennies more numerous, the "You" chant more intense, filling the gym. I wiped my hands and made the shot. Off to a third overtime, which we lost, no thanks to a technical foul by one of my teammates.

So why do I tell that story? Because I will never forget the sight of hundreds of students yelling at me and pointing their fingers, shouting, "You, you, you!" Yes, they were trying to rattle me, but the memory has become a good one for me. Thinking of that game makes me think of Matthew 5:13–14, where Jesus says, "You are the salt of the earth . . . You are the light of the world." I picture Jesus leaning out of heaven right now, but he is lovingly pointing his finger at each of us, saying, "You, you, you, you!"

Jesus wants to use me and you to minister to the men in our spheres of influence. Men who are living in darkness, men who are confused, men who are seeking, men who are wounded, men who are wandering, men who want to grow, men who want to serve, men who want to lead, men who want to make a difference, men who want to be champions in life. Jesus wants to give each of us the "ball," and tells us, "Now it is your time, the game is on the line, the stakes could be no higher. Get in the game and be an impact player for Christ."

Guys, when God breaks into history and grips a man's life, it is with a purpose. People are redeemed by God to serve, to be salt and light. It is inconceivable that God should die for us so that we could be mere spectators until heaven. God has a key role for men to play in the unfolding of his redemptive plans for the world.

Can I be brutally honest with you? I believe with everything in me that we need a calculated sense of urgency about these matters. As you finish this book, go before God and ask him to change your agenda, your plans, and your priorities so they better reflect his love and concern for his people. Some of us are just too busy and caught up in temporal issues to really pour our lives into others. The longer we walk with Jesus, the clearer we should be about eternal realities. Jesus had such a sense of urgency. He was never so absorbed with his own agenda that he forgot about people and the need to invest in their lives.

Life is short. Time is running out. There really is a heaven and there really is a hell. The stakes are forever and God has put you right in the middle of this world to invest your life in others and to awaken the sleeping giant of the church, the country, and the world.

Appendix A

Introductory Materials

IronMan Study from No Regrets Men's Ministries—A nine-week study for those who are looking into Christianity or just getting started.

Men of Change from No Regrets Men's Ministries—Eight lessons to help men learn together about God's standards for life.

Operation Timothy—Four booklets that lay the foundation for new life in Christ.

Man in the Mirror by Pat Morley—Great for starting new men's groups. Covers relevant topics for men.

The Purpose-Driven Life by Rick Warren—Introductory material on being a follower of Christ.

Discipleship Essentials by Greg Ogden—Twenty-four studies to help develop spiritual maturity.

Marriage and Family

Point Man by Steve Farrar—One of the best books on being a spiritual leader in the home.

Great Dads by Robert Hamrin—How to build loving relationships with your kids.

Raising a Modern-Day Knight by Robert Lewis—Provides a guide for dads on how they can guide their sons to authentic manhood.

Anchor Man by Steve Farrar—Provides biblical guidelines for how a father can anchor his family in Christ for the long haul.

Dad, If You Only Knew by Josh Weidmann—What every teenager wants their father to know about growing up.

The Five Love Needs of Men and Women by Gary and Barb Rosberg—Wise counsel for couples on the needs of men and women.

If Only He Knew by Gary Smalley—Great little book that helps men understand the importance of emotional connection in marriage.

Christian Growth

Too Busy Not to Pray by Bill Hybels—Lessons on how to grow your prayer life.

Experiencing God by Henry Blackaby and Claude King—How to know and do the will of God.

Knowing God by J. I. Packer—Looks at different characteristics of God and how you can know him deeper.

Disciplines of a Godly Man by Kent Hughes—One of the most popular men's books ever written.

The Life You've Always Wanted by John Ortberg—An introductory work on the spiritual disciplines.

Lifechange Study Series by NavPress—There is a booklet for each of the books of the Bible.

Prodigal God by Tim Keller—The story of Luke 15 told in a new and challenging way, especially for those who have grown up in the church.

Disciplines for the Christian Life by Donald Whitney—A look at various spiritual disciplines and how to implement them into your life.

Evangelism and Apologetics

Just Walk Across the Room by Bill Hybels—Great book on how to share your faith with others.

The Reason for God by Tim Keller—Apologetic for those seeking and those who want to be able to share their faith more effectively.

How Now Shall We Live? by Charles Colson and Nancy Pearcey—This fabulous book provides the biblical framework for a Christian worldview.

WORK

Integrity by Henry Cloud—One of the best works on the subject. It will keep your group talking and interested for weeks.

The Call by Os Guinness—A phenomenal work on what it means to follow Christ's call on our lives. Every man should read this book.

Your Work Matters to God by Doug Sherman and William Hendricks—One of the best comprehensive books on the subject.

Mastering Mondays by John Beckett—How to integrate your faith and work.

A Man's Guide to Work by Pat Morley—Twelve ways to honor God on the job.

The Fourth Frontier by Stephen Graves and Thomas Addington—Helps you explore the new frontier of work and faith.

Men's Issues

Wild at Heart by John Eldredge—What is a man in today's world?

Tender Warrior by Stu Weber—Practical guidelines for being a man in today's world.

Character Counts by Rod Handley—A great study on accountability, integrity, and what it means to surrender every area of your life to Jesus.

Dream by Kenny Luck—How to tap into God's strength and vision for you.

Risk by Kenny Luck—How to let go and give complete control of your life to Jesus.

Fight by Kenny Luck—How to deal with temptation and the spiritual battle we are all engaged in as men.

Finish Strong by Steve Farrar—Wonderful work on how we as followers of Christ can finish the race we have started. Very practical and insightful.

Battle Ready by Steve Farrar—A study of the lives of Joshua and Caleb and what that means for us today.

God Built by Steve Farrar—A study of the life of Joseph and how God shapes our lives through experiences and relationships.

Every Man's Battle by Stephen Arterburn—Guidelines for protecting yourself from sexual sin.

When Men Think Private Thoughts by Gordon MacDonald—He explores the issues that captivate the minds of men.

Temptations Men Face by Tom Eisenman—Looks at each of the areas that men struggle with today: power, money, affairs, perfectionism, etc.

Leadership

Spiritual Leadership by Henry Blackaby—Great teaching on what it means to be a leader in life.

The Next Generation Leader by Andy Stanley—Learn what it takes to lead with courage and then follow with character. He looks at the five characteristics of godly leaders today.

The Body by Charles Colson—What is the church and Jesus' vision for it?

Equipping Materials

No Regrets Study Series by Steve Sonderman—A new disciplemaking series to equip men to grow deeper in their faith to strengthen their homes, churches, communities, and the world; an eight-book series (8 or 9 lessons per book).

Joshua's Men by Injoy—A twelve-month study that prepares men to be leaders in life.

Leadership Essentials by Greg Ogden—Looks at the various aspects of being a leader in the church and community.

How to Do Men's Ministry

How to Build a Life-Changing Men's Ministry by Steve Sonderman—Practical steps to establishing a ministry to men in the local church.

Effective Men's Ministry by Phil Downer (ed.)—This book provides insights from a number of leading men's ministry leaders around the country.

Why Men Hate Going to Church by David Murrow—Answers the question of why men are leaving the church today.

Brothers by Geoff Gorsuch—How to start and lead effective men's small groups.

No Man Left Behind by Pat Morley and David Delk—A great hands-on book that guides you through the process of developing a men's ministry in your church.

Eternal Impact by Phil Downer—How to disciple a man.

The Master Plan of Evangelism by Robert Coleman—A look at how Jesus built into twelve men that changed the world.

The Accountable Man by Tom Eiseman—Discusses how a small group of men can grow in their accountability to one another.

As Iron Sharpens Iron by Howard and Bill Hendricks—Masterful work on mentoring and how we as men can invest our lives into other young men.

Appendix B

In 1994 we started a ministry at Elmbrook church called Top Gun Ministry with the mission of equipping churches worldwide to effectively minister to men. While our mission has not changed over the years, our name recently has; we are now called No Regrets Men's Ministries. Our mission remains to see every church have a fully functioning and vibrant ministry to men. There are a variety of ways we help men and churches to do this.

1. Conferences/Workshops

No Regrets Men's Ministries presents conferences and workshops around the United States and world to help provide encouragement, motivation, hands-on experience, and training. Each year we regularly hold three separate men's events at Elmbrook Church in Brookfield, Wisconsin. In addition, each of these events can be brought to you to help build up the men of your church community.

No Regrets Conference—This one-day conference is held the first weekend in February. It features two keynote sessions by a nationally known speaker, over forty breakout seminars on topics relevant to what men face today, and live worship by the No Regrets Band. If you are interested in becoming a host-site church, the event can be streamed live to your church. This conference changes men's lives, their families, their communities, and the world. For more information, visit www.noregretsconference.org.

The Man to Man Conference—This workshop equips men to have a personal ministry to men in the context of the local church. The goal of the workshop is to provide an environment where any man ministering to men, whether as a small-group leader, ministry leader, event planner, pastor, or counselor, can be recharged, renewed, and refocused for the work he is doing (www.menwithnoregrets.com).

How to Build a Life-Changing Men's Ministry Conference—This conference is geared to men's ministry leaders in the church. It is best if a number of men from your leadership team attend so you can work through your plan together. This conference works through the nuts and bolts of starting and sustaining a ministry to men in the context of the local church (www.menwithnoregrets.com).

2. Discipleship Resources

No Regrets Men's Ministries is committed to providing tools for men and men's ministry leaders to use in order to disciple the men of their church. Over the years we have written a number of resources that have been used all over the world.

Men of Change Small-Group Study

This eight-week program (no homework) focuses on topics important to men and is designed to get men used to small-group studies. This book is a good way to generate interest in continuing as a group for another book or Bible study.

IronMan Bible Study

The IronMan Bible study is an introduction to Jesus and community. Our desire in writing it was to start a movement of multiplying small groups all over southeastern Wisconsin that are organic in nature.

Our goal through IronMan is to multiply disciples, leaders, and small groups.

It is designed as a vehicle to invite guys who are not yet "there" spiritually into a dialogue that will take them from death and hopelessness into life and community. The aim is to meet in comfortable homes or coffee shops, have easy conversation, allow "wrong answers" and not hit them over the head with Scripture, and, in time, share what Jesus has done for you and what he can offer your new friends. By design, IronMan does not start with group covenants and ask men to pray out loud, using churchy rhetoric. Rather, it attempts to create an atmosphere where every man feels welcome to come as he is into the fellowship of believers.

The first nine lessons (available in booklet form) take guys through the value of doing life together (group life), salvation, prayer, the Bible, temptation, and service. At the end of the nine weeks, men who are grounded in their faith are urged to spin off and start their own IronMan group by inviting friends, neighbors, co-workers, or whomever God has put in their life. Those who are new to faith can continue with sixteen additional weeks of online studies featuring issues common to men.

No Regrets Study Series

Looking back at the men's ministry movement from its roots in the early '90s, we discovered that while there has been some modest success, we are losing the battle for the souls of men in our nation. The need to develop real leadership among our men is greater today than ever. The church needs leaders who can do more than run events. The church needs leaders who know their purpose in Christ. The church needs leaders who can model for men that they are part of something bigger than themselves. We need leaders who can mobilize and encourage men to live life with purpose and with no regrets. This kind of intentional living generates a power that glorifies the Father and can transform an entire faith community. It was with this in mind that I set out to write my newest curriculum, a small-group disciplemaking series to help men to go deep—deep in their relationship to the Lord, deep in their relationship to their spouse, and deep in their relationships to other men. Recently published, the No Regrets series is designed to encourage and equip the men of your church to become authentic leaders in their home, church, workplace, and the world. It has the following characteristics:

1. A *small-group format.* Ten to twelve men per group.

2. A *relational component.* Time for sharing, prayer, and accountability. It is during this time that walls come down and men can be vulnerable with one another.

3. A *righteousness training component.* We aren't just interested in men acquiring more skills, but rather that they attain godliness.

4. A *service emphasis.* The groups do service projects and make commitments to serve within the local church. Additionally, the men do spiritual-gift assessments that help them discover where they should plug into service in their church.

The Purpose of No Regrets

1. *To share life* (1 Thessalonians 2:8–9). The small-group format allows men the chance to be encouraged, challenged, comforted, prayed for, and held accountable. It becomes more than just a sharing of information. It is sharing life with one another. It is a chance for men to develop solid friendships with other men. It is a chance for them to share wounds, dreams, failures, and successes that they perhaps have never shared with anyone else. One of the desired outcomes of the course is that men would see the need to participate in a small-group setting the rest of their lives.

2. *To grow in Christ* (Colossians 2:5–7). It is possible to spend time with other men and never get around to really seeking godliness. The purpose of No Regrets is to help men grow closer to Jesus, to increase their love for him, and to reflect him to the world in which they live. There is a heavy emphasis on the spiritual disciplines and on living a consistent lifestyle. One of the desired outcomes of the course is that men would have a daily devotional time with the Lord.

3. *To be equipped to influence others* (Ephesians 4:11–12). The course is designed to help men discover, develop, and deploy their spiritual gifts. Every man who calls himself a Christian has a spiritual gift. We want to help him find out what it is and then use it to

its fullest. As already mentioned, one of the desired outcomes is that men who have finished the course would serve somewhere in the local church.

How No Regrets Benefits Churches

There are many benefits to starting a small-group study specifically created to equip each member to become leaders in their service to Christ and the local church.

1. *It develops leadership.* When I am consulting with other churches and doing all-day seminars on how to start and run an effective men's ministry, one thing I suggest is that they use No Regrets to develop their leadership. There is nothing wrong with taking a year to develop a nucleus of guys who will be the future leaders of your ministry.

2. *It moves men out of the pews and onto the field.* For many years the only place you would see men serving was ushering or mowing the church lawn. The No Regrets series helps men appreciate the true nature of servanthood and realize that they too have a gift they can use in their congregation.

3. *It starts men growing in Christ.* Men frequently tell me they are tired of just getting together over breakfast and sharing what is new in the world of sports. They say that before they got involved in No Regrets they wanted to grow in Christ but didn't know how. Unfortunately, most men think they are more mature than they really are. The other group has the Peter Pan syndrome—they just don't want to grow up. As a result, men need something to help them cover the basics of Christianity and get grounded in the disciplines of prayer, Bible study, Scripture memorization, solitude, service, and fellowship.

4. *It provides the next step for men after a men's conference or retreat.* One comment I hear regularly in my travels is, "The men's conference/ retreat was great, but when I got home there was nothing." The No Regrets Study series can be described as a men's conference for every week of the year. It is easy for a man to come home from a mountaintop experience like a retreat and settle in to his old lifestyle . . . unchanged. A small-group program set in your

church like the No Regrets Study series can keep a fire originally lit at a conference ignited and the men deepening in their faith.

5. *It starts new small groups.* When a group gets done with the curriculum, we challenge them to stay together and continue on as a small group. We have launched many small groups this way. Because the men have shared together and served together, it is only natural that they become a small-group family. They can meet for an hour or so a week and go through one of the many study books available to men today. No Regrets will be an effective launching pad for your small-group ministry.

For more information on the No Regrets conference, workshops, or the small-group resources from No Regrets Men's Ministries, visit www.menwithnoregrets.com or contact me via e-mail at ssonderman@elmbrook.org

Acknowledgments

Thank you to the men of Elmbrook Church, who have allowed me to use these principles with them for nearly twenty years.

Thank you to the coordinators of the men's ministry who encourage and inspire me through their selfless ministry to others. It is a real privilege to work with each of you.

To Bob and Jon, for running the ministry and freeing me up to lead and speak.

To Stuart Briscoe, my former senior pastor and boss, and most important, friend. Your preaching led me to the Lord almost forty years ago. You called me to serve at Elmbrook some twenty-five years ago, and have given me the encouragement and freedom to do ministry since that time. You are a model of these principles.

To Virgil Staples, the father of men's ministry at Elmbrook. Your early advice to do ministry on men's time, turf, and agenda has been the backbone of everything I do.

To Dave, Mike, and Rob. Your friendship is worth more than gold.

To Dave and Kathy, Phil and Mary, and John and Kris—our couples prayer group. What a joy to have been praying together for twenty years—for our kids and each other.

To Jeff Braun at Bethany House Publishers. Thank you for believing in the project and for your constant encouragement and listening ears.

To Diane, my longtime administrative assistant, who translates my writing, organizes my life, protects my schedule, keeps me humble, and pushes me onward.

To my parents, Lowell and Doris Sonderman. Thank you for being Jesus to me when I was young and telling me about him as I grew up.

To our four incredible children and son-in-law: Kristin, Angela and Kurt, Tim, and Jon. I love you more than you will ever know.

To my wife, Colleen. Thanks for being a godly wife and mother. You are my soul mate and number one cheerleader.

Also from
Steve Sonderman

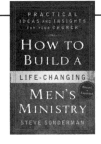

The Leading Book on Men's Ministry Basics

Whether you are starting a men's ministry from scratch or wanting to jump-start an established program, Steve Sonderman gives you the inspiration and practical ideas necessary to take your ministry to the next level—and beyond. In *How to Build a Life-Changing Men's Ministry*, Steve reveals proven ways to reach today's men, including how to

- Plan strategically
- Build effective leadership
- Develop healthy small groups
- Motivate and mobilize your men

Now you can create the vibrant, enduring ministry to men your church needs.

How to Build a Life-Changing Men's Ministry